al

ɔn Kit

Self-Counsel Press
(a division of)
International Self-Counsel Press
USA   Canada

Self-Counsel Press acknowledges the financial support of the Government of Canada through the Book Publishing Industry Development Program for our publishing activities.

Printed in Canada.

First edition: 2002

National Library of Canada Cataloguing in Publication Data
Stuart, Catherine, 1963-
    Simply essential disaster preparation kit/Catherine Stuart.

    (Simply essential series)
    ISBN 1-55180-385-2

    1. Emergency management. I. Title. II. Series.
    HV551.2.S78 2002   613.6'9   C2002-911096-3

Self-Counsel Press
(a division of)
International Self-Counsel Press Ltd.

1704 N. State Street   1481 Charlotte Road
Bellingham, WA 98225   North Vancouver, BC V7J 1H1
          USA   Canada

Contents

WORKSHEETS AND CHECKLISTS 65

Disclaimer

The author, the publisher, and the vendor of this kit make no representations or warranties regarding the outcome or the use to which this kit is put and are not assuming any liability for any claims, losses, or damages arising out of the use of this kit. The user of this kit should not rely on the author or publisher of this kit for any professional advice.

INTRODUCTION

Disasters by their very nature are unforeseeable and devastating. They exact an extensive physical, emotional, and financial toll, and the time it takes individuals and communities to recover from a disaster is often very long.

Consider the following:

- The Loma Prieta earthquake of October 1989 (magnitude 7.1 on the Richter scale) left 62 dead and 3,757 injured. It damaged 18,306 homes, and its financial cost was a whopping 6 billion dollars.

- The Oakland Hills fire of 1991 destroyed nearly 3,000 homes and left 25 people dead.

- The ice storm that affected the New England states and the Canadian province of Quebec in January 1998 left 3.6 million people without power in the middle of a harsh winter. It also left 56 people dead from cold, fire, or carbon monoxide poisoning. In some areas, it was weeks before power was restored.

- Hurricane Andrew of August 1992 left 26 dead and destroyed 125,000 homes. Hurricane Fran, which hit North Carolina in September 1996, left 37 dead.

You cannot know for certain when a disaster will happen, nor can you know in advance how much damage it may cause. You can, however, be prepared.

This simple kit is designed to help you create a family disaster plan, put together a disaster kit, know what steps you can take in a disaster situation to improve your chances of survival, and know what you can do following a disaster to return your life to normal as quickly as possible. The worksheets and checklist section at the back of this book is designed to help you get organized and stay prepared.

Preparation can enhance your chances for survival. It need not be an difficult task.

Start today. Good luck.

1
YOUR DISASTER PLAN

When it comes to disaster, the biggest risk to your survival is having no plan at all. The lack of a plan leaves you and your loved ones at the mercy of events — which, during a disaster, is the worst possible position in which to find yourself. However, if you've thought ahead, you increase your chances of survival and of mitigating any damage that might occur.

It's in your interest to develop a disaster plan.

The following three things are the foundation of any disaster plan:

- Learn the risks for your area
- Prepare your family and your home
- Plot out your evacuation plan

Learn the Risks

What disasters are likely to occur in your area? Chances are, the area in which you live is prone to at least one of the disasters reviewed in Chapter 4. For example, if you live in the south-central United States, tornadoes may be a hazard. If you live on the West Coast, earthquakes are a cause for concern. Ice storms are more of an issue in the New England states, as they are in central and maritime Canada. If you live in an area where floods are possible, the question may be not one of how to prepare for a disaster, but more one of how to quickly and safely evacuate yourself and your family when one occurs.

Find out what hazards may confront you by checking into the history of your area. A good place to start can be with your local branch of the Red Cross or with your local municipal government. Call and ask what disasters may occur in your area and what you can do to be prepared for them. You may also be lucky enough to live in a community that has an emergency-management bureau. Contact them to find out what information and resources are available to the public.

Many cities and townships now have community disaster plans in place. Contact your local city hall and ask for details.

Prepare Your Family and Your Home

If you do the homework suggested above, you'll know what kind of disaster you may have to face. Your next step is to make sure your family knows too, and that they and your home are prepared.

Educating your family involves explaining what might happen and showing each person what he or she can do to prepare. Begin with your dwelling itself. Everyone in your family should know possible exits from the house. Don't limit yourself to doors; ground-floor windows make excellent emergency escape-hatches. You can arrange your furniture so that all these exits can be reached quickly and used by all family members. You can also show everyone where the shut-offs are for electricity, gas, and water, but make certain everyone understands not only how but also under what circumstances to operate them. Show everyone where you keep your first-aid supplies and also where you keep your disaster kit. (Both are discussed in detail in Chapter 2.)

A list of emergency telephone numbers can be a practical as well as a comforting thing to have. These numbers should include the following:

- Fire department
- Police
- Family doctor
- Public health department
- Your and your spouse's work numbers and cell-phone numbers

- Children's school-phone numbers
- An out-of-the-area friend or relative who can act as a check-in for all family members

Post the list somewhere prominent, such as a refrigerator door. (You can use Worksheet 1: Emergency Telephone Numbers, found at the back of this book, to create your list.)

Disasters seldom come with any warning, so you will probably have no way of knowing when one will strike. If your family is, as so many are today, an active, busy one, its very likely that everyone will be in a different place when one does happen. Designate a meeting place outside the home — a place everyone can reach, whether they are at work, school, or a friend's. If a disaster does happen and communication is impossible, your family will still have a way of finding each other. It's a wise move, too, to designate an out-of-state or out-of-province family member or friend as an emergency contact whom everyone can call if local communication is cut off. (It is sometimes still possible to call out of the area even when local phone lines are blocked.)

Disasters of all kinds are often accompanied by fire. You can arm your family against fire now by buying a simple class ABC fire extinguisher (reasonably priced at many hardware and home supply stores) and teaching everyone how to use it. It's also a good idea to have plenty of flashlights on hand — one to be kept in each person's bedroom, if possible — in case of a power failure during a disaster. Remember to keep a stock of batteries, and label the batteries with the date of purchase. If more than a year has passed, replace your stockpile. However, you can avoid the problem of batteries altogether by purchasing crank-operated flashlights, which can be found in some national electronics chain stores.

Have you ever thought about learning some first-aid? Take that course now, or send a family member to it. In times of trouble, 911 tends to be jammed and hospital emergency rooms overloaded. In addition, all should understand the basics of water purification. (See Chapter 6 for more on water.)

You'd be amazed how dangerous simple items found in every home can be when viewed from the perspective of disaster planning. Scour your house for potential hazards, and be skeptical. Secure heavy bookcases to the wall with a simple bracket. (Many bookcases are now sold with such a bracket.) Your hot water heater can be strapped to the wall to prevent it from falling during an earthquake or tornado. If you've got heavy mirrors or artwork hanging over beds, you'll have to put your sense of style on hold and find another place for these items. Pay attention to any object that could fall or break during, say, the high winds accompanying a tornado or hurricane or the shaking from an earthquake. Store chemicals (even such seemingly innocuous things as bleach and household cleaners) in a secure area.

If you know your home needs repairs to its structure, wiring, or ventilation system, there'll never be a better moment than now to do them.

Finally, get out your home insurance policy and really read it, bearing in mind any disaster that may affect your area. If you live in an earthquake zone and don't have earthquake insurance, get it. Earthquake insurance is often considered an "extra," and is not included in a basic policy. Flood insurance is almost never included as part of a regular policy. If you live in a flood zone or an area prone to hurricanes, contact your insurance company to discuss the options. If you live a forested area, you'll have to look at your fire coverage.

Developing an Evacuation Plan

Sometimes a disaster will force you to leave your home, often with very little warning. State and provincial officials have the authority to enforce an evacuation, so you must be prepared to leave quickly.

First of all, ensure that all members of your family know where you keep your disaster kit, because — if you have time to take it — it will be one of the things you'll want to have with you. Keep it in an easy-to-reach place, as you may literally have to snatch it and go.

As your family will likely not all be at home when disaster strikes, the importance of a rendezvous spot is paramount. Make certain everyone knows where to meet.

Making a quick escape will be much easier if you always keep your car's gas tank at least one-quarter full. Keeping a car kit of basic emergency supplies is also a good idea. (See Chapter 2.) Listen to your radio, and take only the routes suggested by authorities, as others may be impassable.

An evacuation will be a lot less stressful if you have an agreement ahead of time to shelter with an out-of-area relative or friend, should a disaster strike. Official shelters are almost certain to be crowded and uncomfortable.

If you do have some time before you have to leave, you may wish to do the following:

- Shut off the electricity. (Unless you are instructed by an authority to do so, do not turn off natural gas. Once it is shut off, only a gas company representative can turn it back on for you.)

- Shut off the water.

- Move garbage cans, children's toys, tools, lawn furniture, and ornaments inside.

- Make arrangements for your pet. Most veterinary associations recommend that you take your pet with you when you evacuate, if at all possible. However, you should be aware that for health reasons, evacuation shelters do not accept animals. If you must stay at an evacuation center, try to leave your pet with a friend or relative whose home is not endangered. If doing this is not possible, the best you may be able to do for your pet is to confine it to a relatively safe part of your house with enough food and water for several days.

Some basic planning will help to make you that much safer. And that bit of safety may make all the difference.

2
PREPARING YOUR DISASTER KIT

Disasters are power and strength gone awry. A hurricane or an ice storm can take out power lines, leaving communities without electricity, and can cause enough destruction to render roads impassable for days. Earthquakes can topple buildings and bring down bridges and overpasses. But just as terrifying as a disaster's strength is the stealth with which some disasters can strike; the first sign of the tornado no one saw coming could be the havoc it causes as it rips through your community at 4 in the morning.

Work and rescue crews may need days or weeks to set your community right again, and it will be up to you to survive in the meantime, and see to your family's need for food, water, and shelter.

You can do it, but you must lay some groundwork before a disaster is upon you. Having a disaster kit ready in advance will help you meet the challenge of survival with a measure of calm.

Luckily, a disaster kit is easy to prepare, and you've probably already got the makings of one there at home. What you don't have now can be purchased at reasonable cost from grocery and department stores.

Take some time now to think about what you'd need to see you through a crisis, and start snooping through your cupboards to see what you've already got on hand.

Survival Supplies

After a disaster, you'll want the following:

- Food and water
- Tools
- Hygiene items
- Physical comfort items
- Medical supplies

Food and water

If an emergency situation occurs, but you are able to stay in your home, plan to consume any perishable food first. You can start with any meat and vegetables you may have in your fridge. If a power outage has occurred, these will be the first foods to spoil. (Meat and dairy products should be discarded if the temperature inside your fridge has been at or higher than 40 degrees Fahrenheit/4.5 degrees Centigrade for more than two hours; vegetable matter can remain edible for six hours.) See Chapter 6 for information on how to prepare food during a power outage.

However, you'll want to stock your disaster kit with food that won't turn on you, and you'll need to keep at least a three-day supply on hand. (**Note:** Some authorities are beginning to recommend keeping enough food in stock for two weeks. Such an amount may be wise, but given the dimensions of the average dwelling, possibly not practical.) Take a hard look at your family's food consumption, then decide how much will keep you going. Remember that your disaster kit is not about ensuring plenty, but rather ensuring survival, and stock it accordingly.

Choosing which foods to include in your kit will take some thought. The food for your kit should be relatively nutritious, but also easy to store. In addition, it should require little preparation. Balancing these requirements may take some doing. Add to that the fact that you'll have to keep in mind any food allergies your family may have, and may have to take into account any medically necessary dietary restrictions. However, all things being equal, here is a list of foods generally suitable to include in a disaster kit:

- Canned meat
- Canned fish
- Canned soup
- Canned fruit
- Canned vegetables
- Canned fruit juices

- Freeze-dried foods
- Evaporated or powdered milk
- Coffee
- Tea
- Bouillon
- Cereal
- Dry pasta
- Dry corn
- Beef or pork jerky
- Rice
- Peanut butter
- Hard candy
- Crackers
- Trail mix
- Beans
- Soybeans
- Salt
- Sugar
- Spices
- Honey
- Vitamin and mineral supplements
- Dry pet food

You will also need to keep to hand the utensils you will need to prepare food. A manual can opener is a must: if the power goes out, that fancy electric opener will be no use to you. You will need a pot, at least one serving spoon, plates (pack some paper or very lightweight plastic plates in your survival kit), cups, and cutlery (again, plastic cutlery is a good option).

For information on preparing food during an emergency, see Chapter 6.

Even more important than an adequate supply of food is an adequate supply of safe drinking water. If a crisis strikes, water supplies may be cut off. Even if the water is still running, there is always a possibility that the water from your tap will not be consumable. Play it safe and keep enough water on hand to see you and your family through at least three days.

As a rule, the average adult will need two quarts (1.9 liters) of drinking water per day. However, deciding how much water to store can get complicated: the hotter the climate, the higher the basic daily ration will need to be. But it doesn't end there. Your kids' water requirement may be even greater, as will that of a chronically ill family member or a nursing mother. You will also need to set aside water for washing and for preparing food. Don't forget that your pets will need a supply of drinking water, too.

Large plastic gallon jugs (available from any camping-supply store) are great for storing water, but make certain that the seal is reliable and watertight. You can store tap water safely this way, but if you are using water from any other source, see Chapter 6 for tips on water purification.

Store your water in a cool, dry place, and do not store any water for longer than six months. Label your containers with the date you filled them. It doesn't pay to take chances.

Tools

It's always a good idea to include certain tools in your survival kit. You never know what situations you may have to face, and being prepared can give you some confidence in the face of a crisis. The following are the basics:

- Flashlight and extra batteries (label batteries with date of purchase), or a mechanically powered flashlight
- Matches (stored in a moisture-proof container)
- Candles
- Wrench (for turning off gas valve, if necessary)
- Pliers
- Screwdriver
- Knife
- Duct tape
- Manual can opener
- Battery-powered radio and extra batteries (or, better yet, a mecahnically powered [crank operated] radio)
- Needles and thread
- Paper or lightweight plastic plates, cups, cutlery
- Small camp-style cook stove and fuel

Hygiene items

Staying clean in a survival situation is not only a challenge, but it's also a necessity. Cleanliness is the most powerful weapon you have at your command in the fight to avoid the diseases that can so easily spread when routines are disrupted and water is in short supply.

Cleanliness is also important to comfort and is a boost to morale when you and your family find yourselves in less-than-ideal circumstances.

To help ensure your hygiene and comfort, make certain your survival kit contains the following:

- Regular bar soap (for use if water supply is adequate)
- Waterless soap (for use if water supply is restricted)
- Moist disposable towelettes
- Sanitary napkins or tampons
- Toilet paper
- Cleaning and storing solutions for contact lenses
- Ordinary chlorine bleach
- Liquid detergent
- Plastic garbage bags
- Paper towels

Physical comfort items

Personal comfort in a crisis really means no more than ensuring you can stay warm and dry. For this purpose, have the following items on hand:

- Sleeping bags
- Blankets (space blankets are ideal)
- A change of clothes for each family member
- Durable, comfortable shoes (no high heels, please)
- Towels
- Extra socks and underwear
- Gloves
- Rain gear and plastic sheeting
- Warm and/or waterproof hats (depending on climate)

Medical supplies

A first-aid kit is a must. You may have one — or at least the beginnings of one — already in your home. Regardless of whether or not you already have one or are putting one together from scratch, ensure that it includes the following:

- Adhesive plasters
- Gauze and adhesive tape
- Scissors
- Antibiotic ointment

- Rubbing alcohol
- Non-prescription painkiller (ASA or acetaminophen)
- Antacid tablets
- Anti-diarrhea medication
- Blister pads
- Iodine
- Latex gloves
- Antihistamine tablets
- Burn ointment
- Sunscreen lotion
- Tweezers
- Thermometer
- Swabs

Also be sure to include any prescription medications you or any family member may need. If you are a glasses or contact-lens wearer, keep an extra pair with your medical supplies. You may need them!

Use Checklist 1 in the forms section at the back of this book to compile your disaster kit, and Checklist 2 to compile your first-aid kit.

For Those Who Are Short on Space

The items mentioned above are those that most authorities recommend keeping in case of disaster. But how realistic are these requirements? What if you live in a small apartment and are short on space?

Decide what the bare minimum will be to ensure your survival, and strive to keep it always on hand. Here are some tips to help guide you:

- Don't skimp on water. Doing so can easily turn a dangerous situation into a deadly one. If nothing else, see to it that you have an adequate water supply. Keep two one-gallon (4-liter) jugs of water on hand. Rotate them into your regular water supply and replace them as you go. (For example, say you have three jugs. When you open one, buy a replacement immediately. That way you'll always have two ready at any time.) You can also fill a couple of

2-quart(or, in Canada, 2-liter) bottles and put them in your freezer, ready to be thawed if necessary.

- Keep in stock several cans of meat or fish and several of fruit or vegetables. These don't take up much space, yet if consumed conservatively can provide enough food to see you though two or three days.
- Don't dispense with your flashlight and batteries, matches and candles, manual can opener, and a knife. These are your essential tools.
- Include your space blanket.
- Cut back your medical supplies to include simply some bandages, a disinfectant, ASA or acetaminophen tablets, and your prescription medications (should you be taking any).

The above supplies will form a bare-bones survival kit, but that just might do the trick for you. It is certainly an improvement on no kit at all.

Use Checklist 3 to compile a bare-bones survival kit.

Storing Your Food Supply and Keeping It Fresh

Storing your emergency food supply need not be a problem. If the food is placed in properly sealed containers, you can store it in your basement — if you're lucky enough to have one that's both cool and dry. If not, try to set aside space in a kitchen cupboard.

Buy some adhesive labels and a marking pen, and use these to label all food with the date as you put it into the basement or cupboard. Every four to six months (absolute maximum), move the food in your emergency supply into your regular supply, and re-place the emergency supply with fresh stock.

Store the food in containers that are designed to keep moisture and pests out. Screw-top glass jars or plastic containers with air-tight seals are acceptable, as are metal cans with re-usable plastic lids, such as coffee cans. Before consuming any food, examine it for spoilage.

Storing Your Emergency Kit

You will want to keep your emergency tools, hygiene and personal comfort items, and medical supplies in one place. A large duffel bag may do for a single person or a couple, but a family may need to be more creative.

One option is to have each member of the family prepare a backpack with his or her own supplies. Another method is to store everyone's supplies in a large, durable container, such as a new or thoroughly cleaned plastic garbage container with a tight lid. You may be able to make space for it in a closet, or if that is impossible, in a dry area of your basement. Try not to resent the space it will take up. If a disaster strikes, you'll be more than glad you made accommodation for it.

If You Have to Evacuate

What should you do if you find yourself in a crisis situation that forces you to leave your home? Evacuation is often necessary during floods and fast-moving fires. Accidents involving hazardous materials, though rare, often force an evacuation. What should you bring?

You may not have much time to think, and you will certainly have none to assemble supplies. In all likelihood, you'll have only enough time to grab your disaster kit and go. If possible, also take as much water as you can carry, as it may be in short supply at any shelter. But the most important thing is not to delay your departure. Remember that evacuations happen only in life-threatening situations. Take the evacuation order seriously and go.

If you have time, be sure to take the following documents along when you leave:

- ID
- Driver's license
- Birth certificates
- Social security card (Canadian residents take Social insurance card)
- Insurance policy

Some bureaus advise taking stocks, bonds, deeds, wills, passports, inventories, etc. You will have to decide what is realistic for your situation. Perhaps the best idea is to make photocopies of all these documents and keep them with your kit.

Do not shut off the natural gas supply before leaving, unless you have been advised to do so by authorities.

You won't be able to evacuate unless you have the means to do so. Keep your car's gas tank at least a quarter full, so that you can make a getaway at any time. Disasters don't announce themselves. They happen without warning.

Car Kit

Some authorities recommend keeping an emergency kit in your car, ready for use at any time. Once again, you will have to decide what your available space will allow. However, it would be wise always to keep the following in your car:

- Flashlight (and batteries, if needed)
- Space blanket
- Maps
- Booster cables
- Cell-phone charger
- Individually packaged granola or energy bars
- Bottled water
- Small shovel
- Small votive-style candles, a deep tin can, and matches

If you live in an area prone to winter storms, you should also keep a bag of salt and some sand or kitty litter (not the clumping kind) in your car, in case you need to gain traction on ice or hard-packed snow. You may want to travel with some extra windshield washing fluid, anti-freeze, and a windshield scraper. Extra hats and gloves may also be life savers.

Checklist 4, at the back of this book, can help you compile a car kit for emergency use.

3
UNDERSTANDING THE WEATHER

Some disasters, such as earthquakes, are impossible to predict. But many, such as hurricanes, tornadoes, floods, and winter storms, are preceded by what the weather service agencies call watches and warnings.

Often there is not much time to take action once the warning signs present themselves. That is why being prepared in advance is to your advantage. But being constantly worried about the possibility of a disaster is unnecessarily stressful and unhealthy. Knowing the warning signs can help you determine when a disaster is likely, so that you need not live life in a permanent state of "maximum alert."

Two of your most useful tools are a familiarity with weather terminology and an understanding of the weather itself. Not all disasters are weather-based, but many are; and in these situations, it pays to have as much knowledge as possible.

Watches and Warnings

Advance information of disastrous weather can often be had by listening to your radio, or paying attention to the television news broadcasts for your area. The National Weather Service constantly observes and analyzes weather conditions across America, and issues bulletins regarding dangerous conditions. (Canadian readers may wish to note that Environment Canada has a similar mandate.) Three useful terms to know are "weather watch," "weather advisory," and "weather warning."

Weather watch

A weather watch indicates that conditions are such that they may give rise to severe weather. A weather watch is your cue for caution. A severe storm, tornado, or blizzard may not yet have manifested itself, but the stage is set for one. When you hear that a weather watch has been issued, be conservative in your judgment. Don't drive unless you must, and stay tuned in to the radio or television for updates. A weather watch does not mean severe weather is bound to develop; only that is it likely.

Weather advisory

A weather advisory means that bad weather conditions are gaining momentum, but are not drastic enough to justify a weather warning.

Weather warning

A weather warning means that severe weather is imminent or is actually happening as the warning is issued. Take shelter immediately. If you are already indoors, stay there until the weather has passed.

Other Terminology

Other weather terminology proceeds logically from the weather watch and weather warning designations:

Winter storm watch: Conditions favor a winter storm. Be cautious about traveling or being outside.

Winter storm warning: A storm is about to happen or is already in progress. Take shelter.

Hurricane watch: This term is usually used in coastal areas. It means that conditions favor a hurricane making landfall within 36 hours.

Hurricane warning: A hurricane packing winds of more than 74 mph (120 kph) will likely make landfall within 24 hours. The warning may remain issued until not only the winds but also the high water and high waves they bring with them have subsided.

Flood watch; flash flood watch: A flood or flash flood is likely.

Flood warning; flash flood warning: A flood or flash flood is about to happen or has actually been reported. You may have to evacuate immediately.

Tornado watch: Atmospheric conditions are likely to give rise to tornadoes. Stay close to shelter.

Tornado warning: A tornado — or sometimes several tornadoes — has been sighted in the area. Take shelter immediately. (Tornado warnings are usually accompanied by information regarding the expected route of the tornado.)

Severe thunderstorm warning: A severe thunderstorm is in progress, causing strong winds, lightning, heavy rain, heavy hail, or tornadoes, or any combination of these conditions. Take shelter.

Blizzard warning: Weather conditions will combine to produce blowing snow, high wind-chill, and extremely poor visibility. Stay indoors. Do not drive.

Cold wave advisory: Temperatures are likely to drop by more than 68 degrees Fahrenheit (20 degrees Centigrade) in the next 18 hours. If at all possible, stay indoors and do not drive.

Judging Weather Conditions

With a little knowledge and some practice, you can become adept at judging weather conditions. Here are some warning signs you can look for:

Tornadoes: Tornadoes occur most frequently during the late spring and throughout the summer, and are more common in the afternoons and evenings. Tornadoes develop very quickly, and are composed of the strongest winds on Earth. They are often — but not always — preceded by thunderstorms that are accompanied by a great deal of thunder and lightning. (Note, however, that a thunderstorm will not necessarily give rise to a tornado.) The sky will usually be quite dark, with greenish-yellow clouds, and the winds may die away completely just before the tornado strikes. There may be a roaring sound. You may notice a funnel cloud, but you should be aware that some tornadoes are almost invisible. You may see only a small cloud of dust and debris kicked up by the point of the funnel.

Floods: If you live in an area prone to flooding, you should become familiar with area's risk. Maintain awareness of snow melt and inches of rainfall, as well as of the relative severity of approaching rainstorms. A flood can take hours to develop, or can happen in minutes. Err on the side of caution.

Hurricanes: Hurricanes may be the only natural disaster for which there is often — though not always — fair warning. Scientists can usually track a hurricane and judge its path well in advance of its landfall. Hurricane season in North America spans from late spring to late fall, and tends to affect mostly the east coast of the United States. If you live in a hurricane zone, your best bet is to listen regularly to weather broadcasts for your area. Often, a hurricane will be preceded by a mild rain shower, a haze around the sun, and an increase in wind.

Winter storms: Winter storms can be difficult to predict from weather conditions alone. Often, they are preceded by overcast skies and moderate temperatures and snowfall, and then come in with a rapid drop in temperature and gain in wind velocity. Sometimes, however, they can begin with relatively sunny skies. If you live in a area that experiences moderate to severe winters, for safety's sake, make listening to weather broadcasts a part of your daily routine. Pay attention to weather conditions not only locally, but regionally. Winter storms have been known to travel quickly.

- *In your car:* Pull over and stop in an area away from tall buildings and overhead structures. If you find yourself on a bridge, however, keep going until you've cleared the bridge, then pull over as soon as you can do so safely. Wait for the shaking to stop before you continue on. Do not use bridges, overpasses, or ramps, as these structures are prone to damage and, after a quake, may be more dangerous than they look. Be very careful of fallen power lines: avoid them!

- *Outside*: Try to get away from tall buildings and other structures and away from power lines. Drop, and protect your head with your arms until the shaking stops.

When the shaking stops

It will feel as if it takes forever to stop, but the shaking is actually over quite quickly. There may, however, be aftershocks. Be ready. Aftershocks are usually not as powerful as the quake itself, but this is not always the case. If an aftershock happens, treat it as you did the quake, Stay where you are until the shaking stops. Be aware, also, that aftershocks can occur days or even weeks following a quake.

Check that the other people in your home are safe. If anyone is injured, administer first aid (that's why you have your first-aid kit and why you took that first-aid course, remember?). If injuries are serious, try calling 911. You may have to be persistent, though, as after even a mild quake 911 is often jammed. There is also a chance that phone lines may be down, however, so be prepared to be on your own for a while.

Examine your home for structural damage. The condition of floors, ceilings, and stairs can tell you a lot about your home's safety. If you see cracks, warpings, loose plaster, or holes, leave immediately. The structural integrity of your home may have been compromised. Stop to grab your disaster kit only if you are certain you can do so safely. Rendezvous with your family members at your pre-arranged emergency meeting place before heading to a shelter or the home of a friend or relative.

If your home has survived, however, here are some tips to help you deal with the aftermath of a quake:

- Put on shoes to protect your feet from broken glass or other debris. Boots are ideal, but thick-soled sport shoes will do.

- Make certain there are no gas leaks. Don't light matches or even flick on the light switches until you're sure the gas lines are sound; this is where your flashlight comes into play. Turn off the gas only if you can smell it or see actual damage to the lines. Remember that once the gas is off, only a gas-company representative can turn it back on.

- Examine your home for fire hazards. Damaged gas and power lines are major causes of fire following an earthquake. The smell of burning insulation may tip you off to electrical hazards, or you may actually see sparks. If so, shut off the electricity, and keep your ABC fire extinguisher at the ready.

- If any household chemicals were spilled during the quake (particularly flammable liquids), mop them up immediately. Once again, do not light any matches until you are satisfied this has been thoroughly done.

- Locate your emergency kit and keep it available.

- Keep your battery-powered or crank-operated radio on to receive news about the quake and about clean-up and rescue efforts.

- Check on your neighbors. They may need help. Alternatively, they may be able to assist you.

- If you have pets, try to find and confine them. The best place for them may be in their kennels until you have your home put right again. Understand, though, that your pets may be frightened and uncooperative. Use as much patience as you can spare.

- Be cautious in cleaning up your home. Protect your hands with work gloves, if you have them. There may be more glass and shattered metal around than you think. Open cupboards and closet doors slowly and with care: you don't want their contents tumbling out on top of you.

And here are some definite "don'ts" following an earthquake:

- Don't return to your home if you suspect it has been structurally damaged. Get professional help to verify that is it safe.

- Don't use the telephone unless you absolutely must. If the system is choked, many people experiencing life-threatening situations may not be able to get a line out.

- Don't flush your toilet if you think sewer lines may be damaged.

- Don't use tap water if you think that your water pipes have been damaged.

- Don't approach downed power lines. Stay at least 10 feet away.

- Don't approach waterfront areas. Tsunamis (massive ocean waves) are sometimes created by earthquakes.

- Do not use your car, unless you have an emergency or are told to evacuate. Ambulances and fire trucks will need to reach people who are trapped or injured, and they will not be able to move if the roads are jammed.

Earthquakes are devastating events, and many people have been injured or killed as a result of them. However, many, many more survive. If you have your disaster kit prepared ahead of time, and can stay calm and use your common sense during the event, you will enhance your chances of staying alive and safe.

Tornadoes

For sheer wind speed, fury, and power, nothing matches a tornado. Tornadoes come packing winds of up to 300 mph (480 kph). They can travel over the ground with breathtaking speed, and their paths are erratic. They occur most often in the states of the midwest as well as throughout the southern states, but can happen anywhere in the United States. Texas, Arkansas, Georgia, Mississippi, Louisiana, Nebraska, Indiana, Illinois, Iowa, Alabama, and Kansas are particularly susceptible. (Canadian readers should be aware that the southern parts of Ontario and Quebec are high-risk areas, as is Alberta and parts of British Columbia, Saskatchewan, and Manitoba.) The United States may experience up to 1,000 tornadoes in any given year.

A tornado can uproot trees, overturn cars, and throw a mobile home off its foundation. But if you take some basic steps to prepare yourself and your home, you can increase your safety and help protect your property

Preparing for tornadoes

Experts generally agree that you are safer inside than you are outside during a tornado. One of the best things you can do, then, to ensure your safety and that of your family is to prepare your home, well in advance of the event, for the possibility of a serious tornado.

Evaluate your home. What can you do to make it more wind resistant? If you live in a tornado zone, installing storm shutters over windows is a good idea. So is checking with an engineer or architect to find out what you can do to reinforce your home's foundation or masonry. Any loose, old, or inadequate roofing should be repaired immediately. Garage doors should also be reinforced.

Take a dispassionate look at your yard. Are there trees that have dead or weak branches? Have these trimmed off now. A tornado could snap them off and turn them into dangerous, even deadly projectiles. Lawn furniture can also be dangerous. At the very least, bring it inside as soon as a tornado watch is issued. The same goes for trash cans. These everyday items can do great damage when hurled by a tornado's powerful winds.

Make certain you and your family are familiar with the terms "tornado watch" and "tornado warning." (See Chapter 3 for more information.)

Designate one room inside your home as your family's shelter when a tornado threatens. The very best place is an area below ground level; if your home comes with a basement, it'll do nicely. If you aren't so fortunate, designate an interior room, preferably one without windows. A bathroom may sometimes serve this purpose, but inner hallways or even closets may be used if necessary. You want to get several walls between you and the wind, if you can do so.

Mobile homes should never be considered secure in a tornado. Be aware that approximately half of all deaths caused by tornadoes occur in mobile homes. Take steps to bolt or tie down your mobile home to its foundation, but understand that it is still likely to be overturned by a tornado. Scout out buildings with good foundations close by in which you can seek shelter.

Keep your disaster kit in an easily accessible place, and keep a battery-powered or crank-operated radio on hand. You should also check with your municipality or township to discover what warning systems are in place.

Check with your children's schools to make certain they have a designated safe area and that they periodically practise tornado drills The same goes for your workplace. If there is no tornado plan in place in your children's schools or your workplace, start one yourself. This is another move that will pay off in peace of mind.

Weather services will issue tornado watches and warnings whenever possible when conditions warrant, but tornadoes can be very quick to develop — sometimes too quick to be reported. In the Canadian province of Ontario, a popular camping spot was struck by a tornado in July 2002. By the time it was visible on radar, it had already touched down. Your best defense is always to be prepared.

When a tornado watch is issued

Tornadoes can happen at any time of the year, but they are most common from May through September, and most tornadoes occur in the afternoon. Get into the habit of monitoring weather reports on television and radio, especially if there are or recently have been thunderstorms in your area. When a watch is issued, here are a few things you should do:

- If possible, cancel any travel plans. Don't put yourself in any situation in which you might be caught outdoors or in a car. A truly powerful tornado can throw a car hundreds of feet.

- Quickly bring in any lawn furniture, trash cans, etc. Store them in your basement until the watch is over. If you don't have a basement, store them in a room other than your designated shelter room.

- This is the best time to bring pets indoors — provided you don't have to spend hours outside searching for them. Confine them to one room or to their kennels.

- Close your windows and doors. The idea that a closed-up house will explode if struck by a tornado is a popular misconception — and a dangerous one, at that. On the contrary, great damage occurs when high-speed tornado winds gain entry to a house, bringing debris with them. This is exactly what you want to avoid.

When a tornado warning is issued

All right. The warning has been issued, which means that tornadoes have actually been spotted in your area. Or maybe you've actually seen the funnel cloud yourself. What now?

You have no time to waste.

Do the following:

- Go to your designated room. The reason you have designated one in advance is so that you won't have to think about it now.

- If your designated room has a window, stay well away from it.

- Keep close to the center of the room. (If you are in a bathroom or closet, this won't be an issue.) A tornado's winds usually kick debris into the corners of a room, so you want to avoid them. If you can, wrap yourself in a blanket to help shield you from flying glass. It may even help cushion the impact of flying objects.

- If possible, duck under a strong piece of furniture, like a heavy table or desk, and hold on. (If the tornado's winds do find their way into your house, holding on may help to keep you in one spot.) Otherwise, simply crouch down, protect your head with your arms, and hope for the best.

- Do not leave your designated room until the winds have subsided.

If you aren't in your dwelling when a tornado hits, try to remember these suggestions:

- *Outside:* Try to get to shelter. If no building is nearby — or near enough to reach in time — get to the lowest ground available — a ditch will do — and lie down. Cover your head with your arms.

- *At work:* If a basement is available, go there. If not, get under a desk or worktable. Cover your head with one arm, and hold on with the other. Stay out of rooms with wide-span roofs, such as cafeterias and warehouses. The roofs of such places, as they have no supporting walls in the middle, are particularly vulnerable.

- *In a car:* Don't try to outdrive a tornado. Often, they can move much faster than a car. Besides, a tornado's path is often erratic, and sometimes there can be more than one tornado. Get out of your car and into a building, or get out of your car and well clear of it and lie down on the lowest ground available. Once again, a ditch will do.

After the tornado has passed

Once you are certain the winds have died away and the danger has passed, come out of your designated room cautiously. With a little planning and luck, your home will have weathered the storm. The following suggestions are meant to help you deal with the immediate aftermath:

- Check with family members to discover if anyone is injured. Administer first aid. If injuries are serious, call 911. Understand, however, that if phone lines are still working, 911 may be flooded with calls. Call only if injuries are life threatening.

- Check your home for structural damage. You'll be looking for cracks, holes, and warping in the ceilings, roofs, stairs, walls, and foundations. If you have any reason to believe that your home is unsafe, leave immediately.

- Check gas, power, and water lines. If damaged, shut them off immediately. (Note, however, that it's foolish to try to shut off electricity if you have to stand in water to reach the circuit breaker. Call an electrician.) Do not light matches or turn on light switches until you have verified the soundness of the utility lines.

- Be alert to the possibility of fire; it is common following disasters. Keep your fire extinguisher handy. This is what you got it for.
- Check on your neighbors.
- Start your clean up by putting on sturdy shoes and work-gloves. Mop up any chemicals or flammable liquids that may have been spilled. Take special care in cleaning up shattered glass. There's always more of it than first appears.
- Use your battery-powered or crank-operated radio to monitor emergency broadcasts. If your power lines are not damaged, you can use your television.

Hurricanes

Hurricanes are birthed off the cost of Africa. They travel across the Atlantic Ocean to the Caribbean and the Gulf of Mexico, often hitting the states of Florida, Louisiana, and Texas. However, all the states of the east coast can be affected, and even eastern Canada may experience hurricanes from time to time.

A hurricane is a cyclone, an immense storm of ferocious wind circling at speeds of more than 74 mph (120 kph) around a center of stillness, called the eye of the hurricane. A hurricane may be several hundred miles in diameter, and in addition to its violent winds, also carries extremely heavy rains and a phenomena called storm surge: the winds can raise enormous waves at sea that build on their way toward land, becoming 20 feet (6.5 meters) or more in height and dozens of miles wide. Storm surge can flood a coastal community with an unimaginable amount of water, leaving death and destruction in its wake. A hurricane can also create tornadoes, and landslides can sometimes follow in the wake of the heavy rain accompanying a hurricane.

Concern has been growing over America's preparedness — or, in fact, lack thereof — for hurricanes. Data from the National Oceanic and Atmospheric Administration suggests that hurricanes are less frequent now than they were in the middle decades of the 20th century, but the general consensus is that this decline in frequency is only a lull. Hurricane frequency will inevitably rise once again. Compounding this problem is the fact that the population of the east coast has risen dramatically in the last few decades. This area also attracts hundreds of thousands of tourists and vacationers every year. However, improvements to the road systems have lagged behind the population boom. Authorities often tell people to move inland before a hurricane strikes, but the quick and efficient evacuation of such a large population is becoming more and more of a problem.

What can you do to protect yourself and your family?

Preparing for a hurricane

Hurricane season in the United States stretches from May to November, so begin your preparations long before that. Don't wait until a hurricane watch has been issued to lay in extra food and water; by that time there will be line ups at the stores, which may be out of what you need or closed altogether. Start now.

The first step is similar to the first step mentioned above in the section on tornadoes: evaluate your home, asking yourself what can you do to make it more storm resistant. Install hurricane shutters to protect your windows, and try checking with an engineer or architect to find out what you can do to reinforce your home's foundation or masonry. Any loose, old, or inadequate roofing should be repaired immediately. Take a good look at your rain gutters and downspouts. Are they large enough to handle a great volume of water? Have them cleaned and make certain they remain unblocked. Garage doors should also be reinforced.

Now examine the property surrounding your home. If the trees have dead or weak branches, trim these off now. You don't want a hurricane's high winds to snap them off and hurl them against your house. If you have lawn furniture, make a mental note to bring it inside as soon as a hurricane watch is issued, along with your trash cans. Left outside during a hurricane, these items can cause all manner of mayhem.

If you live in a mobile home, ensure that it is securely tied down. Be aware, however, that this precaution is no guarantee against it being overturned in hurricane-force winds. If you live in a mobile home, you should arrange to shelter somewhere more secure.

You and your family should understand the terms "hurricane watch" and "hurricane warning." (See Chapter 3 for more information.)

Do a little homework with a map, and plot out several possible routes inland, in case you have to evacuate. One of the worst things you can do when an evacuation order comes is to jump in your car in a panic and start driving without a clear idea of your route. You should also familiarize yourself with where the hurricane shelters for your area are. You local branch of the American Red Cross may be able to provide you with this information.

You may not be advised to evacuate, so you should choose one room in your house where you can either wait out the storm or stay until the order to evacuate comes. If possible, choose an interior room or hallway without windows or skylights. Don't try to shelter in a basement during a hurricane. Basements have a well-deserved reputation for flooding.

Have your disaster kit ready to hand. If you receive the order to evacuate, you'll want to be able to just grab the kit and go. This is a good time to make certain you have extra provisions on hand and also to increase your stock of bottled water. Safe water is the number-one non-negotiable requirement of life, and following a hurricane, it can be in amazingly short supply. If you take any prescription medications, always keep at least a two-week supply in your home throughout the hurricane season.

Make sure you have enough flashlights and batteries, and ensure that the batteries all work by putting them in the flashlight and turning it on and off. Make certain, also, that you have a battery-operated radio and a good supply of working batteries for it. If you have a crank-operated radio, ensure that it is in working order.

Keep your car fueled up. You may have to evacuate (you almost certainly will, if you live on the coastline or an island, in a floodplain, on a landslide-prone slope, or near a river), and if you do, gas will be in very short supply and you will not want to waste valuable time at the pump.

It's a good idea to keep a stash of cash available. In the aftermath of a hurricane, financial institutions may be closed and ATMs may not be serviced or even functioning.

You may feel as if you're going to a great deal of trouble for very little reason. But it will take only one hurricane to make you know how necessary it all is.

When a hurricane watch is issued

Once a hurricane watch has been issued, it's time to step up your preparations. Here are some suggestions:

- Fold up your lawn furniture and stash it inside, along with all trash cans and anything else that could be blown around.

- Make sure your pets are inside. Once you have them inside, don't let them out again. The darkening sky, along with the increased wind and the noise it creates, can frighten your pet and cause it to find its own hiding place outside — which will probably be much less safe than indoors with you.

- Secure the storm shutters over your windows. Inside, pull down the blinds or draw the curtains to cover up the window from the inside and help prevent shattered glass from being blown inside. (Taping windows may help to keep glass fragments from flying through the air if storm winds break a window, but it is no substitute for shuttering or boarding up your windows.)

- Set your refrigerator and freezer to the lowest temperature possible. If the power goes out, having done so will help to keep food a bit longer. You may want to consider buying bags of ice to put in your freezer to help keep the temperature down.

Keep listening to radio and television for weather bulletins as they are issued. They can give you a great deal of information regarding the behavior of the storm as it approaches and the need to evacuate.

An evacuation will sometimes be ordered during a watch for particularly susceptible areas. If you are in such an area, take the evacuation order seriously.

When a hurricane warning is issued

First, and most important, if you are ordered to evacuate, leave immediately.

But until that order comes, here's a game plan:

- Stay tuned to radio or television broadcasts. Make sure you have your battery-powered radio in case you have a power outage.

- Move valuable documents and items to the top storey of your house to minimize the possibility of them being damaged by flood waters. You may want to put your documents in watertight containers. Whatever your choice, keep them handy so you can grab them quickly if you must evacuate.

- Make certain you have enough drinking water to see you through at least a week. Fill up bottles and jugs. Some agencies recommend filling your bathtub. You'll have to decide if this is a practical move for you.

- This event is what you bought your flashlights for. Keep them close by.

- Don't shut off utilities, unless advised by officials to do so.

- You may experience a power failure. Unplug your appliances. Otherwise, they may be fried by power surges when the juice comes back on. (Don't forget to unplug your computer and all peripherals, including the monitor.)

- Move to your designated hurricane room, and make yourself as comfortable there as you can. You could be there for a long time.

Stay inside until it's truly over. Sometimes, people mistake the eye of the hurricane for its end. In fact, if the eye passes over you, you will have a period of calm before the wind and rain comes screaming back from the opposite direction. No one can tell how long this period will last, and it can be quite short, so going outside during this phase of a hurricane is foolhardy. Many people are injured or killed doing just that. Don't be one of them.

When you have to evacuate

When you have to evacuate, you, of course, won't panic. You began preparing for this a long time ago, back at the beginning of the hurricane season, when you studied your map for the best routes away from your area. You already know where the shelters are, because you've checked in advance. Alternatively, you know you'll head to the home of a friend or relative who lives comfortably inland — 30 to 50 miles — because you and your friend or relative have already discussed and agreed on such an arrangement, and you called your friend or relative back when the watch was issued to confirm it. Your disaster kit is already assembled and ready for you to throw in the car, along with your important documents and cash stash, and you've been keeping your car gassed up all along.

You're well ahead. You'll probably beat the herd out of town, and be safer for it.

Now, the most important thing for you to do is not to delay when the evacuation order comes. The longer you wait, the more likely it is that you'll encounter choked roads on your way out of town. If you haven't already done so, bring in all lawn paraphernalia and shutter your windows. Shut off your electricity at the main circuit breaker, and shut off the water at the main valve. Lock your doors and hit the road.

Many authorities recommend calling a contact outside your area so that someone knows of your plans. By all means, do so if it will not cause a delay. But you may want to make the call from some convenient place along the road. Alternatively, you can have a companion or family member make the call from a cell phone while you drive.

Do not return to your home until authorities have advised you it's safe to do so. Why takes chances? In any case, you'll have to wait until all obstructions have been removed from the roads and the roads are driveable again. Be patient. The state of emergency will not last forever, and life will resume as normal once again.

When the hurricane's over

If you remained in your home during the hurricane, the first thing to do in the aftermath is to check yourself and your family for injuries. Administer first aid (you're glad you took that course, aren't you?), and call 911 only for life-threatening emergencies. Check on your neighbors, too. If possible, make an agreement with them before disaster strikes that you will look in on one another. Your neighbors will be able to reach you following a disaster much more quickly than a rescue crew will.

Next step: examine your home for damage. Check roof, walls, and as much as you can of the foundation from the outside. If you find cracks, missing pieces, holes, or if any part of the structure appears to be sagging or leaning, you'll know that the building's integrity — and therefore its safety — has been compromised. Leave immediately. You will need the help of a building contractor and possibly an engineer to make it safe once again.

Check the area immediately surrounding your home for downed power lines. If you find any, stay well away from them but notify the power company. These lines are a fire and electrocution hazard.

If your home is surrounded by water, do not enter (or re-enter it). That water is putting pressure on your home's foundations — quite literally squeezing them. Wait for the water to recede before going back inside.

Now examine your home from the inside. Use flashlights, rather than candles or lanterns. Once again, you are looking for cracks, holes, and sagging in the floors, ceilings, and walls. Pay attention to staircases as well. If you find evidence of damage, clear out immediately, and get a professional's advice regarding the extent of the damage before you attempt to resume living there. You don't want to take a chance on having your home collapse on you.

Pay attention also to the condition of your home's electrical system. If you smell overheated wire insulation, or see sparks or damaged wires, shut the system down from the main circuit breaker. You may want to contact an electrician to ensure that your system is safe to use. If you detect the scent of leaking gas, immediately turn off the gas at the main valve and, as soon as you are able, inform your gas company. Be cautious, also, about sewage and water lines, as these are often damaged during hurricanes.

If your home is still structurally sound, you'll probably nonetheless be facing a major clean-up effort. Here are a few things you'll need:

- Swamp boots
- Heavy, protective work gloves (several pairs would be best)
- A good supply of detergent and disinfectant
- Plenty of mops, sponges, rags, and scrubbing brushes
- Pails or buckets
- Plenty of garbage bags

The flooding that accompanies a hurricane is a major concern. Flood waters often carry sewage with them, so everything that flood waters have touched must be either disposed of or disinfected. (For more information on floods, see the section on floods in this chapter.)

Be very careful as you sift through any debris. Many a person has discovered that snakes or rodents have taken refuge inside from the hurricane. It's best not to risk being bitten.

Open all the windows to let the air circulate and help your home dry out. If your basement has been flooded, you must pump the water out gradually, over a period of a few days. Pumping the water out all at once could cause basement walls to cave in under pressure from the soaked earth outside. Take your time with this crucial task.

Sort through your refrigerator and freezer and throw out any spoiled food. If you're not certain about the condition of a specific item, be ruthless. Dispose of it.

Do not use tap water for drinking or cooking until you are assured by authorities that it is safe to do so. For information of purifying water, see Chapter 6.

Allow electrical equipment and appliances to dry out thoroughly before attempting to see if they are usable again. This may take up to two weeks.

Keep listening to your radio for updates on the situation in your area.

The clean-up following a hurricane is a heavy job. You may be without electricity and drinking water for days, even weeks. For tips on getting through this period, see Chapter 6.

Floods

Water is amazingly powerful. A small amount of it can be relatively heavy, and when moving rapidly, quite destructive. Floods can occur at any time of the year, but are most common in spring or following atmospheric disturbances such as heavy rainstorms or hurricanes Snow melt is a great factor in many spring floods; if a winter of only moderate snowfall is followed by unusually hot weather in the spring, the resulting melt may cause flooding.

Certain areas are more prone to flooding than others. Floodplains (flat or low-lying land along the bank of a river or other body of water) are aptly named and are not the best places to build dwellings, but are populated nonetheless. Valleys in areas subject to moderate or heavy snowfall can be flood prone. Floods have occurred in virtually every state in America. In Canada, flooding is most likely to occur in parts of Manitoba and Quebec but can affect other provinces as well.

Flash flood — floods that can build to destructive levels in only hours or even minutes — generally follow on the heels of earthquakes, ruptured dams, hurricanes, tsunamis, or unusually heavy rainfall.

Landslides sometimes accompany floods, and much of the information that follows is applicable to landslides.

Floodwater is not something to be trifled with. Fast-moving floodwater of no more than ankle depth has enough force to topple you over; if it's of mid-calf depth, it can drag you along in its current. Eighteen to 24 inches of floodwater on the move can take your car along with it.

A flood is far more powerful than you are. Your best bet is to put your energy into mitigating the damage floodwaters may do to your property and into developing a solid evacuation plan.

Preparing for a flood

Because of the nature of floods, you may not get a great deal of warning that one is developing. It's worthwhile for you to learn whether or not your community has ever been flooded, and especially to learn if your dwelling lies in the flood path, and make sure you know what your community's warning system is. You can usually get this information from your local municipal or township government, the local branch of the Red Cross, or your local emergency-response agency.

Some authorities suggest keeping some building supplies on hand, such as lumber and plywood, plastic sheeting, a hammer and nails, shovels and sandbags. Unfortunately, you may have neither the warning nor the time to make use of these things before a flood occurs. A good defensive move would be to talk to a plumber about installing check valves in all your sewer traps to keep floodwaters from flowing into your home through your drains. Talk also to a structural engineer about what you can do to reinforce you home's foundations, as they are the part of your home most susceptible to damage from a flood. If your main circuit breaker, furnace, or water heater are in your basement, you may want to get some advice regarding how you can relocate these to an area of your dwelling where they are more likely to stay dry.

Make sure you and all members of your family are familiar with the terms "flood watch" and "flood warning." Be certain, also, that you and all members of your family know how to shut off your utilities, as you may have to take this step immediately prior to evacuating.

Don't wait until a flood watch or warning to develop your evacuation plan. Floods will leave you very little time to make a getaway. Plot out at least two paths you can take to high ground, and keep your car gassed up. In the event of a flood, gas will be in very short supply. Know where you are going before a flood ever develops. If you can, make an agreement with a friend or relative who lives on higher ground and who can put you up if the need arises. Alternatively, know where the shelters are in your area.

As always, keep your disaster kit up-to-date, and in an easily accessible location. You should also keep your important documents and some cash at the ready, so that you can grab these things and leave if you must.

When a flood watch is issued

Once you've been notified that a flood in your area is possible, don't delay taking action. The flood may not develop, or you may be very lucky and it will pass you by, but you can't take that chance. Instead, take some action:

- Stay tuned to radio or television for updates on the situation.

- Get as much as you can carry of your furniture, artwork, and valuable items to the top storey of your home. It will all have a better chance of surviving undamaged up there. Don't forget your computer.

- Find your pets and get them inside. If you have to evacuate, keep in mind that shelters will not allow you to bring your pets. Make arrangements to leave them with a friend who lives outside the flood area. If this is not possible, the best you may be able to do for them is to confine them to a room on the highest level of your home, with plenty of food and drinking water.

- Drinking water may not be available in the days following a flood. Now is the time to stockpile. Fill empty containers, your sink, and even your bathtub.

- Fold up your lawn furniture and store it inside. Don't forget the trash cans.

- Be ready to shut off your utilities if instructed to do so.

- If you have not had check valves installed in your sewer traps, you can try to plug your drains with corks or wooden plugs. It's better than nothing. Floodwater can back up via your toilet, so you'll have to remove it to plug the connection.

Notice to evacuate may be given during a flood watch. Don't ignore it. Floods have a habit of moving very quickly, and you must take the opportunity to get away while you can.

Flood warning and evacuation

If a flood warning has been issued, you'll know that a flood is developing in your area. Flood warnings are usually accompanied by an order to evacuate.

Because you'll already have made preparations to leave, you can do so immediately. Shut off your utilities if instructed to do so, take your disaster kit, and go. The more you delay, the higher the floodwaters may become, thereby decreasing your chances of getting out of the area safely.

The order to evacuate may be accompanied by recommendation on which route to take to higher ground. Follow these recommendations, as other routes may not be passable due to rising water, and don't be tempted to drive around barricades. You may find floodwaters already rising and blocking your route. Do not drive through them. Find another route.

If you are unfortunate enough that your car stalls in rising water, get out of the car and leave it in the lurch. Run to higher ground as fast as you can move. Don't try to get your car started again or to move it by manpower. Such a move could cost you your life (and your car isn't worth that much, is it?).

You may be unlucky enough to be caught outside during a flood. If this happens, your choices will be extremely limited. Do not try to cross floodwaters on foot (or in a car, for that matter) and don't fool yourself that you can swim through them, as they will likely be much stronger than you are. Get to high ground as fast as you can.

After the flood is over

Don't return home until you know it's safe to do so. Floodwaters may take days to recede, and even when they do, you cannot return to your house again to live until all the floodwater around it has evaporated and all the water in it has been removed. You have a big job ahead of you.

First of all, wait for any floodwater around your home to recede. You can't go back in until the flooded land around your house is relatively dry again. The pressure the water-soaked earth places on your home's foundations can cause them to buckle and collapse.

Check your home for structural damage. Look for cracks and holes in the foundations, walls, and roofs. If you find evidence of structural compromise, call in an engineer or building contractor, but don't attempt to resume living in your house until repairs have been made. The same goes for inspecting the inside of your home. Enter with flashlights (not candles or lanterns; if flammable substances have washed into your house, you risk a fire), and protect yourself from both contaminated floodwater and electrocution by wearing rubber boots and rubber gloves. Check the inside walls, ceilings, floors, and staircases for damage. Look for cracks, holes, sagging, or leaning. If you have any reason to think your home may be unsafe, do not stay inside. Get the repairs done first.

Check for gas leaks. If you smell gas, turn the gas off at the main valve and leave your home immediately. Call the gas company for advice. If you didn't turn off the electricity when you left, do so now, but only if you can reach the circuit breaker or fuse box without having to stand in water. Some experts suggest standing on a dry wood block or board and turning off the main switch with a dry stick, but you are probably better off calling in an electrician rather than attempting such a maneuver.

A flooded basement means you must pump the water out gradually over a period of at least three days. Trying to do it more quickly than that could cause the foundations to collapse. Don't rush this job. Don't risk your home or your safety.

If you have a septic tank, check it before you start flushing your toilets again. If you suspect that the flood has got the better of your sewage system, have it repaired as soon as you can.

You are ready to start your clean up. You'll need the following:

- Rubber boots and rubber gloves for everyone involved
- Pails
- Mops, sponges, rags, and scrub brushes
- Non-ammonia detergent
- Bleach
- Garbage bags
- Masks (for protection against mold and fumes (dual-cartridge respirators are best)
- Shovels (for removing mud and debris)

Sad though it may be to admit, your home at this point is a health hazard. Floodwaters are often contaminated by sewage. Rotting food is a breeding ground for bacteria. Soaked furniture, carpets, bed linen, etc., will begin to grow mold if not cleaned and dried out quickly. You'll have to act fast, but because of the size of the job ahead of you, you'll have to pace yourself accordingly.

Be cautious during your clean up. Snakes and rodents can travel with the floodwaters right into your home — where they can give you an unpleasant surprise, at best, and a nasty bite at worst. They can also be sanitation hazards, so be on the alert.

Here are some basics to start you on your way to getting your house back in order:

- Get your house dry. Open all doors and windows to let the air flow through. If all standing water has been removed, you may be able to rent industrial fans to help speed the drying process.
- Take your shovel and start mucking out all the silt and debris.
- Examine your walls for the flood line (the highest point the floodwaters reached). If the floodwaters entered your house, it'll be obvious to you where the line is. Measure a good two feet above it: you now have the unenviable task of removing and replacing all the drywall from there down. Your drywall has been soaked with contaminated water, and no, you really can't live with it. The same goes for the insulation behind it.

- Clean your walls and all surfaces that may have come into contact with floodwater. Use your bleach for this purpose, and be sure to rinse when you've finished. Surfaces that have not been directly touched by floodwater should nonetheless be cleaned using a four-parts to one-part mixture of water and bleach. Once again, rinse when you've finished.

- Flooring can present a particular problem. You'll have to make an assessment. The water and bleach solution may do to clean flooring that has not been directly touched by floodwater, and you may be able to clean and quickly dry out carpeting in the same situation. However, if your linoleum, carpeting, or other flooring has been truly soaked or under floodwater for any period of time, your safest move is to replace it. Don't delay removing your carpet and underlay. The combination of contaminated water and mold is a serious health risk.

- It will be hard to do, but you'll have to discard certain items if they have been soaked by contaminated floodwater, including upholstered furniture and mattresses.

- Clean away dirt and silt from floor drains, then pour in some bleach to disinfect them.

- Allow all electrical equipment and appliances to thoroughly dry. This may take up to two weeks. Cautiously test them before using them again.

- Sewage systems are often flood casualties. Do not flush your toilet until you are certain your sewage system is up to the job.

Because power failures commonly accompany floods, food spoilage is a real hazard. There's also the danger that foodstuffs may have come into contact with floodwaters. Play it safe, and consume only canned foods following a flood, but be sure to disinfect the cans before you open them, and throw away any cans that have been dented. Don't trust bottles or jars, either. Bacteria carried by floodwaters has a way of crawling in under the lids. Throw them out.

Absolutely do not drink your tap water or use it to prepare foods unless the authorities have advised you that it is safe to do so. Do not use it for washing your hands, either. The water supply is frequently contaminated after a flood, and the water company and health officials need time to deal with this problem. For information on how you can purify water, see Chapter 6.

It is a very good idea to decontaminate your dishes, cutlery, pots, and pans following a flood, even if they have not been directly touched by floodwater. Allow them to stand for a half hour in a solution of one part bleach, four parts water, then rinse and dry them.

Winter Storms

In the winter of 1998, the Canadian city of Montreal was struck by an ice storm that shut the city down for weeks, left thousands without power, and left many dead. Winter storms are a reality throughout most of the United States and all of Canada, and cause more deaths than other disasters. It pays to be prepared for them.

Preparing for winter storms

If you live in an area prone to winter storms, start preparations well before the storm season arrives. (For most of North America, that means in September or October.) You should see to both your home and your car at this time.

To prepare your home, take the following steps:

- Winterize your doors and windows. Caulk and weather-strip them to prevent heat from escaping. You'll be more comfortable, and you'll love what it does for your heating bill. Storm windows are always desirable in winter. In a pinch, you can also use plastic sheeting layered over the inside of your windows. Staple it to the window frame, then use a hand-held hair dryer to melt the plastic around the edges to provide an air-tight seal.

- Check your home's insulation. If your insulation is not adequate, upgrade it before the cold weather arrives. Once again, you'll be much more comfortable, and you'll be pleasantly surprised by your heating bill.

- If your pipes haven't been insulated, do it now. The insulation will help keep them from freezing. (Frozen pipes are a disaster all on their own.)

- Keep a good stockpile of heating fuel.

- Make certain your roof is strong enough to handle the burden of a heavy snowfall. If necessary, install structural supports.

- Keep your flashlights and extra batteries on hand. There may be a power failure, and being cold and in the dark is a truly depressing situation.

- Keep your disaster kit handy and up-to-date.

You should get your car ready for the cold weather, too. If necessary, enlist the aid of a trained mechanic:

- Ensure that your battery, starter, heater, brakes, four-way flashers, and radio are all in good working order. If you get caught in a blizzard, you're going to need them all.

- Your cell phone could very well be your best friend if a storm blows up while you're on the road. Have a charger installed in your car.

- Keep a supply of washer fluid and antifreeze ready.

- Splurge on tires. Buy the best ones for winter driving conditions that you can afford.

- Keep your car disaster kit in your car at all times. (For more information on assembling a car disaster kit, see Chapter 2.)

- Always make sure your car is gassed up. Avoid running low.

When a winter storm watch is issued

A winter storm watch has been issued, so you know that the chances are high that a storm will blow into your area. Perhaps the temperature is already dropping, and you can hear the wind picking up. What should you do at this point to stay safe?

Try the following:

- Consider all travel plans carefully for the next 24 to 36 hours. (Travel plans include even mundane things such as trips to the grocery store.) Do you really need to go out? If so, go sooner rather than later, and don't dawdle on your way back. Storms have a habit of blowing up quickly.

- Get your pets inside. If a storm hits when they're outside, they may not be able to make it back to you, and you don't want to be wandering around outside in a blizzard looking for Fluffy. And believe it or not, your average house cat will freeze to death in a blizzard. Don't take that chance. Once inside, keep your pets there. (Cat owners may need to keep a kitty-litter box on hand for these occasions.)

- Stay tuned to radio and television broadcasts for updates about the weather.

When a winter storm warning is issued

The storm's really going to happen, or has already begun. What should you do now? It's mostly a matter of waiting it out. But here are a few commonsense tips:

- Avoid going outside. The blowing snow that accompanies winter storms and blizzards can reduce visibility to nothing, and render even familiar ground unrecognizable. You've probably heard at least one story of a person freezing to death within a few yards of his or her own home. It happens, so don't let it happen to you.

- Stay tuned to the radio and television broadcasts about the weather, and have your battery-powered radio handy in case your area experiences a power failure.

- If the storm show signs of settling in for any length of time, consider turning down your home's heat to save fuel.

- Keep your flashlights, batteries, and disaster kit in an easily reached place. Also have some votive-style candles and a couple of deep tin cans (empty coffee cans are best) handy to provide warmth if the power goes out.

- You may want to leave your faucets open just a touch to keep water flowing through your pipes, which can help keep them from freezing. Frozen pipes often swell and burst when they thaw — a messy and expensive situation.

- If you are forced to go out, make it quick, and don't stray far from your home. Dress for the occasion: put on a hat. (It may look uncool, but it could help to keep you from freezing to death.) Wear mittens (not gloves), and wrap a scarf around your mouth so you won't be breathing in freezing air. If you're shoveling snow, stop and rest from time to time. Lots of people have had heart attacks from the combination of extreme cold and exertion brought on simply by trying to keep their walkways and driveways clear.

If the power goes out

It's a bad situation, but not necessarily desperate. Don't expect to be comfortable, but there are a few things you can do to make your situation more bearable:

- Add some layers to your clothing. Make sure the layer next to your skin is an absorbent, natural fiber, like cotton. Put on a hat; an unbelievable amount of body heat is exhausted through the head.

- Unplug appliances and electrical equipment to avoid a power surge when the juice comes back on. Turn light switches off.

- Do not open the doors to your refrigerator or freezer, unless absolutely necessary. Opening these appliances lets cold air into your home — which is just what you don't need — and can cause your food to spoil that much more quickly.

- Retire to one room, preferably a bedroom. Keep the door closed. If there are drapes or blinds over the windows, close them too. Doing so will help keep heat from escaping the room more quickly than it must and can help keep cold from getting in.

- Light your votive candles and set them in your deep tin cans. The candles will generate some heat; not enough to keep you toasty warm, but enough to stave off freezing. **If you are alone, you must blow out the candles before going to sleep. If you are with other people, take turns sleeping, but do not leave the candles burning with no one tending them.**

- Do not use barbecues of any kind or camping cookstoves in your home. The fumes will kill you. Authorities regularly issue warnings regarding this hazard, and every year, someone dies foolishly by disregarding the warnings.

- Leave one light turned on, so that you'll know when the power has been restored.

When you find yourself on the road and your car stalls

Well, but this isn't supposed to happen. If you followed the advice above, you'll know that the truly storm-wise stay at home during severe weather. But it may happen that you'll find yourself in this predicament. There are a few things you can do to make the situation a little less dangerous:

- Always travel with your car disaster kit. The space blanket, extra hat and gloves, bottled water, and energy bars may make all the difference to you.

- If you have a cell phone, take it with you when you travel. If you get stranded, call someone to let him or her know your approximate location.

- Put your four-way flashers on. It will help make you more visible to approaching cars.

- Don't leave your car. Attempting to hoof it to find help is among the most dangerous things you can do. The blowing snow of a blizzard can reduce visibility to zero, and you can easily lose your bearings, and the extreme cold can impair your ability to think clearly. Your chances for survival are much greater if you remain with your vehicle. Wait for help to find you.

- Run the engine for about 5 minutes every half hour or so. When you do so, open a window just a bit on the leeward (away from the wind) side of the car. If snow is piling up outside, periodically check to make sure that it isn't blocking your exhaust pipe.
- Drink some of your bottled water. The extreme cold can lead to dehydration.
- Stretch and move your arms and legs from time to time. Doing so will stimulate your blood flow, which will help to keep you warm.

When the storm is over

There's always a feeling of relief when the wind and the driving snow of a severe winter storm have died down. You must remember, however, that the temperature outside may still resemble that of the Antarctic. You can venture outside, but use a little caution.

Check the area around your home for downed power lines. If you find any, keep well away from them and report them to the power company.

Offer assistance to you neighbors, if they need it. They may not have weathered the storm as well as you have.

Take you time when it comes to clearing the snow from your walkway and driveway. Overdoing it with the shoveling can lead to heart attack; every year, someone dies this way, too.

Be patient when it comes to getting back on the road again. It may be quite a while before roads are safe to drive. Let the authorities do their work of snow removal before taking your car out.

Sometimes a blizzard will be followed by hours of dazzling sunshine and remarkably clear air. Take some time to enjoy the sight. It really is beautiful.

Wildfire

There are few things more frightening and more rapidly and entirely destructive than fire. Wildfires may start in wilderness or wooded areas, but can move with devastating speed, encroaching on rural dwellings and even city suburbs. In the right area, a wildfire on the rampage can take out hundreds of homes.

Experts advise us to design and build our homes with the possibility of fire in mind, but how practical is this advice? Most of us rent or buy homes that are already built. Often, it's more realistic

— not to mention very wise — to consult the local fire marshal, along with a reliable building contractor, to see what can be done about retrofitting a home with fire-resistant material. And, of course, smoke detectors are indispensable.

However, we all do have some control over our surroundings. If you live in an area that could be threatened by wildfire, there are things you can do to reduce your risk. Here are a few suggestions:

- Trim your trees. Cut back branches so that their tips are at least 15 feet (5 meters) from your house, garden shed, and garage. Trim off the lower branches entirely, so that the first branches on the trees are 6 feet (2 meters) off the ground. Doing so can keep a ground fire from rising into the treetops, where it will be truly uncontrollable.

- Keep an ABC fire extinguisher on each floor of your home. These are readily available from many hardware and home-supply stores, and are reasonably priced.

- Have a good look at your garden hose. Can you wrap it completely around your house? If not, get one that's longer. You must be able to get water from the outlet to any part of your house or yard in a hurry. (And if it's summer, keep the hose hooked up to the outlet all the time. You never know.) Don't forget to stock a ladder that's high enough to give you access to your roof. You may find yourself up there some day, desperately hosing down the shingles. (By the way, did you have them treated with fire retardant? Tile or metal roofing is much safer than wood.)

- Get out your rake. Keep your yard and surrounding area free of all combustible bric-a-brac: leaves, twigs, dead grass, etc. If you have a lawn, keep it well watered and mowed to within a half-inch of its life.

- Clean out your gutters, or have it done for you. Keep them clean throughout the long, hot summer. Pine needles, dead leaves, etc., are a fire just waiting to happen.

- Swap your wooden lawn furniture for metal. (Plastic will not do; it burns hotter and more toxically than wood.)

- Construct your very own fire break. Doing so needn't be as dreadful a task as it sounds, and the fire break itself needn't be an eyesore. A nice flagstone or gravel path meandering about the circumference of your property could potentially be just enough to interrupt a fire's path. Some experts also advise installing a pool or pond to create a safe zone around your home; nice, if you can afford it.

- If you have any option in the matter at all, and if you can do so safely, run the lines for electrical utilities underground.

- If you must, alter your grounds, driveway, or yard so that it's easy for the firefighters to approach your home. A location at the end of a long lane or driveway may afford privacy, but can be hell for a fire truck to negotiate. To accommodate fire vehicles, have your lane or driveway widened to about 16 feet (20 is even better), and make sure the trucks will have turnaround room once they get to your house. Keep the lane or driveway clear of overhanging branches.

It should go without saying that you've developed a family disaster plan, as described in Chapter 1. Review it at the start of the fire season, and refresh everyone's memory regarding routes out of the house and out of the neighborhood and numbers to call. Your disaster kit should be up-to-date and in an easily reached location. You'll have little, if any, time to spare if a fire strikes.

When a fire is burning in your area

This may be one of the most frightening situations you'll ever face. Put your family on alert that they may have to leave in a hurry.

You'll need to keep yourself informed. Stay tuned in to radio and television broadcasts, and keep a battery- or crank-operated radio handy in case the power fails.

Take the following precautions *but only if time allows*. If the danger is immediate, you must leave that instant:

- If you can do so quickly, get your pets inside. Put them in their kennels, so that you can just grab them and leave if you must evacuate.

- Set yourself up for a fast getaway. Park your car in front of your house (*not* in the garage). Throw your disaster kit in the back, and keep the car keys with you so there's no fumbling around when it's time to go.

- Close all doors and windows and any non-flammable window coverings you may have, but remove draperies.

- Shut the gas valves.

Some agencies suggest setting a sprinkler on the roof, but you'll have to decide if this is practical.

Act promptly if the order to evacuate should come. Lock your doors and go. Ideally, at the start of the fire season you will have arranged shelter with a relative in another area. Call if you can do so safely. The best way is to make a call from a cell phone while you're on your way.

When the fire's over

Natural though it may be to want to return home quickly, wait until you get the word from the authorities. Keep listening to news broadcasts for information. When you do return, here are a few things to keep in mind:

- There may be a great deal of dust and ash in the air. Keep your dust mask handy. Put on boots and heavy work gloves when you begin your clean up.

- Roofs often remain a danger zone, even seven or eight hours after the all clear has been given. Some agencies suggest hosing down your roof as a precaution. At the very least, you should scope out your roof for smoke, smoldering, embers, or any other sign of trouble. Take a good look inside your attic as well, and then go over the rest of the house carefully. You'll have to do this several times in the hours following your return home.

- Check your yard. Are there any dangling power lines? If so, don't go near them and don't leave them unreported. Call your power company. If any of the poles look as if the fire got the better of them, don't approach them, either, as they may be about to fall. Once again, let your power company know immediately. Burned trees may also be a problem; their structure has been undermined, and you may have to have them removed.

- Be wary of your tap water. Don't assume it's safe until you've been so informed by authorities. See Chapter 6 for information on purifying water.

5
TERRORIST ATTACKS

Terrorist attacks are among the most unpredictable of disasters. They are planned and executed in stealth. Unlike hurricanes, floods, and wildfires, there is often absolutely no warning, and the attack itself may take many forms.

Prior to the attacks on the World Trade Center and the Pentagon on September 11, 2001, terrorist attacks were almost unknown in the United States. However, with the high death toll from the events of that single day, terrorism in America has become a fact of life.

What can you do to keep yourself and your family safe? As with any emergency, there is no method that guarantees survival. But there are actions you can take to help you increase your chances of coming through a terrorist attack.

Must-Have Supplies

Having a pre-assembled disaster kit is more important than ever. If the water supply is attacked, you must have ample water on hand to meet your needs. Food may suddenly become difficult to obtain if supermarkets shut down or if supply routes are disrupted, so any canned food you've put aside will be worth its weight in gold. The same goes for medical supplies.

Take another look at Chapter 2 to review how to assemble a disaster kit. Use common sense and keep your own space requirements in mind, but whatever your situation, don't skimp on your supply of bottled water. The following is a list of other "must haves" in addition to your water and food supplies:

- *Flashlights and lots of current batteries, or a crank-operated flashlight:* The power may go out, and it may stay out for a long time. Being frightened is bad enough, but being frightened in the dark is more than you should have to bear.

- *Battery- or crank-powered radio:* By now, the value of this item in any disaster will be obvious. In the event of a terrorist attack coupled with a power failure, it will be your only way of getting any information on the situation. Authorities will broadcast information on the nature of the attack, its extent, whether you should stay or leave, and possible evacuation routes. Being informed could save your life.

- *Dust masks:* Dual-cartridge masks are best, and are available from many hardware and home-renovation supply stores. Be certain you have enough for your whole family. The dust from the collapse of the World Trade Center towers presented a serious health hazard for weeks following the attack.

- *Fire extinguisher:* A simple ABC fire extinguisher is available from most hardware and home-renovation supply stores. Learn how to use it (this takes about 10 minutes) and teach the rest of your family.

- *Duct tape and plastic sheeting:* Great for covering window areas if the glass gets blown out.

- *Boots and heavy work gloves:* Shattered glass and toxic debris are a real threat following an attack. Protect your hands and feet.

- *A stash of cash:* Be wily, and keep some "real" money socked away with your disaster kit. Following an emergency, your credit cards may be useless. The electronic equipment for swiping cards may not be working (ditto for automated banking machines), and shops may not be open in any case. There may be people who have goods you desperately need and who are willing to part with them, but only for cash.

Do some serious thinking. Is there anything else that forms a basic to your survival or that of a family member? Do you have any special medical needs? Carefully consider what is essential, then undertake to have these items always on hand.

Preparedness Strategies

Review your disaster plan with your family. (For information on developing a family disaster plan, see Chapter 1.) Make sure everyone knows the phone number of the out-of-town relative or friend to call in case of disaster, and that everyone knows where to meet if returning home is not possible. You should also make certain school authorities know how to contact you, and that your children themselves have your work (and cell) phone number, as well as your out-of-town emergency-contact number.

It's always a good idea to arrange to shelter with an out-of-town friend or relative in case of an emergency. Official shelters will be very crowded and uncomfortable.

Don't forget your pet. Plan now for what you'll do with Fluffy or Fido should an attack happen. If you must evacuate, take your pet with you. Many of those who were forced to evacuate the area around the World Trade Center left their pets behind, never dreaming that it would be weeks before they could go home again. Official shelters will not take pets due to health regulations, so make alternative arrangements.

An excellent preparedness strategy is to take a first-aid course. It will give you the information — not to mention the confidence — you need to deal with various injuries, and could very well be a life saver in the aftermath of an attack, when hospital and medical services will be stretched past their limits.

If you've prepared a disaster plan, you'll already have identified at least two ways out of your home. If you live or work in a high-rise building, however, get to know all the exits. Find out where the stairwells are, then take each and every one of them all the way up and all the way down so that you'll know where they terminate. The last thing you need when you want to get out of a building fast is to end up in the parking garage. Don't let yourself in for any surprises. Make a mental note of where the fire extinguishers are, and read the instructions on how to use them.

In addition, identify all possible routes you can take home if an emergency is declared, and all possible routes to your family's emergency meeting place.

Learn all the exits from any public building or mall you frequent.

When an Attack Happens

An attack can take many forms, from explosions to the release of chemical or biological weapons. Because it's impossible to predict what type of attack may occur, it's impossible to set out a plan of reaction similar to the ones for hurricanes or winter storms. What follows, however, are a few basics that might help.

Follow the directions of the authorities. If told to evacuate, do so. Collect your family and pets, grab your disaster kit if you have time, lock your doors, and go. If you are advised to do so, shut off your water and electricity. You may want to inform an out-of-area friend or relative of where you are going, but don't waste valuable time. You may be able to make that call while you are on your way. If you have a cell phone, have a companion make the call while you drive.

If the authorities tell you to evacuate in a certain direction (i.e., "North" or "West"), do so. Chemical and biological weapons are often designed as aerosols to disperse in the direction the wind is blowing.

You may be told to "shelter in place." If you receive this instruction, stay home. Shut your doors and windows and turn off your air-conditioning system, heating system, and any fans. If you can, move to an interior room without windows, like a bathroom, but don't go to the basement. You may be sheltering against a chemical or biological agent that is heavier than air and which will sink down rather than rise. Keep your battery-powered radio with you so that you can listen for further instructions.

If an explosion occurs in your building, get out as fast as you safely can. If your way is blocked, however, your choices will be extremely limited. The best you may be able to do is to shelter under a sturdy piece of furniture and wait for rescue workers to come to you. Stay down by the floor as the air at that level may be less hazardous to breathe (smoke tends to rise). Grab the front of your shirt and cover your mouth and nose. It's better than nothing.

Tactics for dealing with the release of chemical or biological agents are problematic, owing to the nature of these attacks. It may, in fact, be some time before anyone is aware that an attack has occurred. However, once discovered, such attacks will likely be accompanied by an order to shelter in place. Use your duct tape to seal up the cracks around doors and windows, and await further instructions.

Be prepared, but do not let the fear of a terrorist attack rule your life. Have your plan in place and your supplies on hand, then go about your daily life, knowing you've done all that is possible.

6

SURVIVAL: WATER AND FOOD AFTER THE DISASTER

After a major disaster, your most immediate needs will be your most basic: water, food. This chapter gives you some suggestions on how you can provide these things — safely — for yourself and your family.

Water

It's impossible to do without water, but after many disasters, safe water is in very short supply. You, of course, will have enough bottled water put by to see you through a crisis, because you've prepared a disaster kit.

But what if it isn't enough? Or, worse yet, what if you didn't set any aside before the disaster?

You are in dire straits, but not quite without options.

Finding water

There's probably some right there in your home. You'll have to treat it to purify it, but it'll do. Look in the following places:

- *Your freezer:* You have ice cubes in there, don't you? That's water. Thaw it out, and you'll be able to drink it with no further ado. You may also have bags of crushed ice. Thaw it and drink up.

- *The tank of your toilet:* It's not a very appetizing idea, but this water is usable. Just don't drink it or use it for cooking until after you've purified it. (See the section below on treating water.) Water in the toilet bowl, however, remains completely out of bounds. Don't even think about it.

- *Your water heater:* If your water heater hasn't been touched by floodwater, you can use the water stored there. Once again, you'll have to treat it before you do anything with it. (See below.) It's a bit of a pain to get the water out. Shut off the gas or electricity first, and shut off the water intake valve, then open the valve at the bottom of the tank.

You can also turn to nature. You can collect rain water, but make certain the containers you collect it in are scrupulously clean. Water from ponds, streams, or rivers may also be usable (once again, you'll have to treat it), but be careful that no sewage or floodwater has washed into whatever body of water you're plundering. If you suspect it has, or are even just unsure, don't use this water.

Treating water

None of the water from any of the sources above should be considered safe as is, and in fact, there's no way to make it 100 percent safe to use. But there are a few methods that can make it less hazardous. You're aiming to try — as much as possible — to kill most of the bacteria and microbes that may be in the water.

The old stand-by method is to boil the water for 10 minutes, then let it cool. You'll lose some of your water as it vaporizes, but this method has for centuries been a tried-and-true mode for rendering water drinkable

Plain old bleach (the non-perfumed, chlorine kind, which, of course, you have on hand in your disaster kit), can be used to treat water. Take one quart of water and mix in four drops of bleach. (Canadian readers, take one liter of water and mix in four drops of bleach.) Allow the water to sit for half an hour. It's the chlorine in bleach that does the work. Alternatively, you can obtain chlorine-based water-purification tablets from many camping-supply stores. Follow the directions carefully.

If you have no other choice, you can use iodine to purify water, though iodine is not deemed to be anywhere near as effective as chlorine bleach. Try 10 drops to a quart (10 drop to a liter), and hope for the best.

All these methods have their shortcomings: there may be some microbes that survive the treatment, and these methods cannot remove heavy metals. Distilling the water is the only other alternative, but bear in mind that even this method has its limits. As mentioned above, nothing is 100 percent certain.

Distilling in post-disaster conditions is rather difficult and will not yield you much water. Some authorities recommend filling a pot to the halfway point, then taking the lid, tying a cup to the handle of the lid, then flipping the lid over so that the lid is inverted and covering the pot. (You have to ensure, somehow, that the water in the pot doesn't flow into the cup.) Bring the water to a boil and let it boil for half an hour. The vapor that condenses on the inverted lid will, as it collects, drip into the cup as water — distilled water. You'll have to decide if this method is a possibility for you.

You may be able to adjust your diet so that your body's water requirements are not at peak. For instance, consume more carbohydrate and less protein, and don't drink any coffee, tea, or alcohol (all of which deplete the body of moisture). But don't attempt to go without water. You simply can't do without it.

Food

No matter how great the upset a disaster causes, you will still need nutritious food. But, as with the need for water, this basic requirement also is fraught with problems. The two thorniest questions will be "Is my food supply safe to consume?" and "How can I cook it?"

Safe food

Your disaster kit is packed with food that keeps well (i.e., canned, dried) and which you've been replacing at regular intervals. This food will form your main supply for the next few days.

Of course, there may also be food in your refrigerator. If your area hasn't had a power failure, you can consume this food as you normally would. However, if the power has gone out, it's a different story.

Many foods spoil surprisingly quickly, even at a moderately cool temperature like 45 degrees Fahrenheit (7 degrees Centigrade). You won't see it or smell it, but after about 2 hours at that temperature or higher, a bacterial explosion occurs in meat, fish, milk, cream, and soft cheeses, rendering them unsafe for consumption. The same goes for foods such as soups, casseroles, and even leftovers. You'll have to throw these items out.

Better news might be found in your freezer, though. If the freezer is relatively full of well-frozen food, that food may last as long as two days. Strictly limit the number of times you open the freezer door, and once the food starts to thaw, either cook it immediately or throw it away, hard though that may be to do.

There are a few foodstuffs that will keep relatively well. Most fruits will survive two days without refrigeration. Breads and peanut butter will be O.K. for the same amount of time as well. There are some who say that hard cheeses will keep for a couple of days at room temperature (68 degrees Fahrenheit; 20 degrees Centigrade) and that eggs will keep for the same time if in a cool place. But your watchwords must be caution and common sense. For example, if you're suffering through the humid dogs days that often follow hurricanes in the south, none of the items mentioned above may be safe to eat.

Keeping a good supply of disaster-kit-style food on hand is your safest option.

Cooking food if the power is out

If you want to cook food, but your electricity isn't yet working, you have a few choices.

Gas or charcoal barbecues will do nicely, but as mentioned in Chapter 4, never operate barbecues or grills indoors. The effect is lethal. The same goes for camp stoves. All these choices can be used only outside.

However, if you have a fireplace, and if your chimney has been left untouched by whatever disaster has struck, you can cook there, albeit very carefully. Try using this option only for small, unambitious meals. An indoor fireplace is usually more ornamental than practical, and yours probably hasn't been designed for cooking ease.

A fire in the backyard is really not recommended, as it can be hard to contain and may be an outright violation of fire regulations for your area. Do you really need more trouble?

If you have none of the above, but have a chafing dish, that will be better than nothing. You can use it to warm small amounts of food.

Ration your cooking fuel. There's no telling how long you'll be without electricity. Cook only those foods that truly need it.

7

YOUR PROPERTY AND POSSESSIONS

If you are like most people, nothing matters to you more than your own life and well-being and the lives and well-being of your family. But if you are like most people, you may also have a certain affection for your home and possibly even have one or two prized possessions with which you would never want to part and that you would never want to see damaged. This chapter deals with protecting these items. There are steps you can take both before and after a disaster to mitigate your losses.

Before a Disaster

You owe it to yourself and your financial health to discover which disasters are likely to occur in your area, and then to do what you can to lessen the effect such disasters might have on your life and property.

Many of the measures you can take to secure your property and possessions before a disaster are described in Chapter 4. For instance, if you live in an area prone to hurricanes, you may be able to mitigate the damage such an event could do to your home by reinforcing its foundations, strengthening its roofing, and installing storm shutters. If you live in an area prone to winter storms, you should ensure that your home is adequately insulated and that your roof is strong enough to handle the weight of a heavy snowfall.

In addition to these steps, however, it is always a good idea to secure all documents attesting to your home's value (and that of your possessions), and to inventory your possessions.

Get yourself a safety deposit box, and use it to keep documents such as your home-ownership papers, your insurance policies, and any appraisals or receipts for items such as jewelry, antiques, or expensive electronic equipment. (You may be required to prove the value of these things in order to collect insurance on them.) You may also want to keep other documents here, such as investment certificates and, of course, your inventory of your possessions.

Inventorying your possessions means simply making a list of everything of material value that you own. Along with listing the item, note also its approximate value (you may want to keep receipts — if you have them — with your inventory) and the approximate date you acquired the item. If the item has a model or serial number, note this too. When it comes to more expensive items, such as antiques or jewelry, it's always a good idea to take a photograph in addition to listing the item on your inventory. Doing so provides you with visual proof of what the item looked like originally, which could be useful in proving the item's value should it be damaged in a disaster. Use Worksheet 2 (found at the back of this book) to compile an inventory of your possessions. (*Simply Essential Family Records,* also published by Self-Counsel Press, can provide you with all the forms you need to organize and document your possessions and vital family information.)

Many insurance companies suggest that you include in your inventory things such as table, bed, and bathroom linen, as well as clothing. When taken altogether, these things can be expensive to replace.

It is also useful to visually document the pre-disaster condition of your home. You can do this quite easily by taking photographs of the exterior of your home (photograph all four sides) and of all the rooms of your dwelling. Once again, such records may serve you well should you have to make an insurance claim.

Of course, it is crucial that you have adequate insurance. It could be the single most important tool in helping you recover from a disaster. A disaster is devastating enough all on its own, but just think of how you'd feel if it left you facing financial ruin.

Insurance

Whether you own your home or rent it, you need insurance.

If you own your home, ensure that you have home-owner's insurance, and that it covers full replacement. You may have to have your home appraised from time to time to ensure that the replacement cost specified in your policy matches your home's current value, but this expense will be well worthwhile should a disaster strike. If you do any renovations or home improvements, make certain your policy takes them into account. Check also how much you will have to pay in deductible before your policy kicks in, and find out whether or not your policy will cover the cost of your living expenses should you be forced to vacate your dwelling. You can't afford unpleasant surprises in this area. Be certain that your policy also includes coverage for the replacement cost of your possessions.

If you rent your home, you are not without responsibility when it comes to insurance. You must have your own insurance to cover your possessions, no matter what your landlord's arrangements are. Check the deductibles to make certain they are acceptable, and find out whether or not the policy covers any expenses should a disaster force you to locate elsewhere while repairs are being made.

Understand that it is very likely you will have to purchase extra insurance to cover specific disasters, such as earthquakes, hurricanes, floods, and tornadoes. **Don't assume your policy includes this coverage; in all likelihood it does not.** It's your responsibility to ensure that you are adequately covered. If you live in a disaster-prone area, you must speak to your insurance company to find out the details of disaster-specific coverage.

After a Disaster

In the chaos that often follows a disaster, you may have trouble deciding what to do first. However, if your home or possessions have been damaged, it's important that you call your insurance company as quickly as possible to get the claim process rolling.

Getting through to your insurance company may take some time and effort. Be persistent. You owe it to yourself. When you do get through to your agent, note down any instructions and be certain to follow them. If your home is damaged, the insurance company will have to send out an adjuster to assess the damage, but if you must make repairs immediately to make your home livable, ask your agent what repairs will be acceptable so that you do not do anything that might complicate your claim.

Photograph the damage to your home and possessions, and retrieve your inventory so that you can present it to the adjuster with the photographs.

If the disaster has forced you out of your home, be sure to keep any receipts for lodging. Depending on what kind of coverage your policy provides, you may be able to make a claim for such expenses, but you must provide proof of how much you spent. In addition, if you have had to relocate, let your insurance company know how to reach you.

The period following a disaster is stressful and heart-wrenching. Knowing that you are adequately insured and having the documentation to prove your claim can make all the difference to you at this time.

Worksheets and Checklists

- WORKSHEET 1: EMERGENCY TELEPHONE NUMBERS
- CHECKLIST 1: DISASTER KIT
- CHECKLIST 2: MEDICAL SUPPLIES
- CHECKLIST 3: BARE-BONES SURVIVAL KIT
- CHECKLIST 4: CAR KIT
- WORKSHEET 2: CONTENTS OF HOUSE CHECKLIST

WORKSHEET 1
EMERGENCY TELEPHONE NUMBERS

Fire department   _____

Police   _____

Family doctor   _____

Public health department   _____

Work and cell-phone numbers

    Office   _____

    Office   _____

    Cell   _____

    Cell   _____

Children's school numbers

    Child 1   _____

    Child 2   _____

    Child 3   _____

    Child 4   _____

Out-of-area check-in   _____

Insurance company   _____

CHECKLIST 1
DISASTER KIT

Date: _____

Food and Water   # of units

- ❑ Water   _____
- ❑ Canned meat   _____
- ❑ Canned fish   _____
- ❑ Canned soup   _____
- ❑ Canned fruit   _____
- ❑ Canned vegetables   _____
- ❑ Canned fruit juices   _____
- ❑ Beef/pork jerky   _____
- ❑ Freeze-dried foods   _____
- ❑ Evaporated or powdered milk   _____
- ❑ Coffee   _____
- ❑ Tea   _____
- ❑ Bouillon   _____
- ❑ Cereal   _____
- ❑ Dry pasta   _____
- ❑ Dry corn   _____
- ❑ Rice   _____
- ❑ Peanut butter   _____
- ❑ Hard candy   _____
- ❑ Crackers   _____
- ❑ Trail mix   _____
- ❑ Beans   _____

- ❏ Soybeans _____
- ❏ Salt _____
- ❏ Sugar _____
- ❏ Spices _____
- ❏ Honey _____
- ❏ Vitamin and mineral supplements _____
- ❏ Dry pet food _____

Tools

- ❏ Flashlights _____
- ❏ Extra batteries _____
- ❏ Matches _____
- ❏ Candles _____
- ❏ Wrench _____
- ❏ Pliers _____
- ❏ Screwdriver _____
- ❏ Knife _____
- ❏ Duct tape _____
- ❏ Manual can opener _____
- ❏ Battery-powered or crank-operated radio _____
- ❏ Extra batteries _____
- ❏ Needles _____
- ❏ Thread _____
- ❏ Paper or lightweight plastic plates, cups, cutlery _____
- ❏ Cooking pot _____
- ❏ Camp-style cook stove _____
- ❏ Fuel _____

Hygiene Items

- ❑ Regular bar soap   _____
- ❑ Waterless soap   _____
- ❑ Moist disposable towelettes   _____
- ❑ Sanitary napkins or tampons   _____
- ❑ Toilet paper   _____
- ❑ Cleaning and storing solutions for contact lenses   _____
- ❑ Ordinary chlorine bleach   _____
- ❑ Liquid detergent   _____
- ❑ Plastic garbage bags   _____
- ❑ Paper towels   _____

Physical Comfort Items

- ❑ Sleeping bags   _____
- ❑ Blankets (space blankets are ideal)   _____
- ❑ Change of clothes for each family member   _____
- ❑ Durable shoes   _____
- ❑ Towels   _____
- ❑ Extra socks   _____
- ❑ Extra underwear   _____
- ❑ Gloves   _____
- ❑ Rain gear   _____
- ❑ Warm and/or waterproof hats   _____

CHECKLIST 2

MEDICAL SUPPLIES

Date: _____

	# of units
❑ Adhesive plasters (mixed sizes)	_____
❑ Gauze	_____
❑ Adhesive tape	_____
❑ Scissors	_____
❑ Antibiotic ointment	_____
❑ Rubbing alcohol	_____
❑ Non-prescription painkiller (ASA or acetaminophen)	_____
❑ Antacid tablets	_____
❑ Anti-diarrhea medication	_____
❑ Blister pads	_____
❑ Iodine	_____
❑ Latex gloves	_____
❑ Antihistamine tablets	_____
❑ Burn ointment	_____
❑ Sunscreen lotion	_____
❑ Tweezers	_____
❑ Thermometer	_____
❑ Swabs	_____

CHECKLIST 3
BARE-BONES SURVIVAL KIT

Date: _____

	# of units

❏ Water ⎯⎯⎯⎯⎯

❏ Canned meat ⎯⎯⎯⎯⎯

❏ Canned fish ⎯⎯⎯⎯⎯

❏ Canned fruit ⎯⎯⎯⎯⎯

❏ Canned vegetables ⎯⎯⎯⎯⎯

❏ Flashlight ⎯⎯⎯⎯⎯

❏ Batteries ⎯⎯⎯⎯⎯

❏ Matches ⎯⎯⎯⎯⎯

❏ Candles ⎯⎯⎯⎯⎯

❏ Manual can opener ⎯⎯⎯⎯⎯

❏ Knife ⎯⎯⎯⎯⎯

❏ Space blanket ⎯⎯⎯⎯⎯

❏ Adhesive plasters ⎯⎯⎯⎯⎯

❏ Disinfectant ⎯⎯⎯⎯⎯

❏ ASA or acetaminophen tablets ⎯⎯⎯⎯⎯

❏ Prescription medications ⎯⎯⎯⎯⎯

❏ Bleach ⎯⎯⎯⎯⎯

CHECKLIST 4
CAR KIT

Date: _____

# of units

- ❑ Flashlight _____
- ❑ Batteries _____
- ❑ Space blanket _____
- ❑ Maps _____
- ❑ Booster cables _____
- ❑ Individually packaged granola/energy bars _____
- ❑ Bottled water _____
- ❑ Small shovel _____
- ❑ Votive-style candles _____
- ❑ Deep tin can _____
- ❑ Matches _____
- ❑ Cell-phone charger _____
- ❑ Salt, sand, or kitty litter _____
- ❑ Windshield washing fluid _____
- ❑ Anti-freeze _____
- ❑ Windshield scraper _____
- ❑ Extra hats and gloves _____

WORKSHEET 2

CONTENTS OF HOUSE CHECKLIST

[*List only those items that you wish to keep a record of. Those items that are of no sentimental or dollar value, need not be included.]

ITEMS	INSURED Yes No	ORIGINAL COST	DATE OF PURCHASE	REPLACEMENT COST	PHOTOGRAPH ATTACHED

FURNITURE

_____	❑ ❑	_____	_____	_____	_____
_____	❑ ❑	_____	_____	_____	_____
_____	❑ ❑	_____	_____	_____	_____
_____	❑ ❑	_____	_____	_____	_____
_____	❑ ❑	_____	_____	_____	_____
_____	❑ ❑	_____	_____	_____	_____
_____	❑ ❑	_____	_____	_____	_____
_____	❑ ❑	_____	_____	_____	_____
_____	❑ ❑	_____	_____	_____	_____

BLINDS & CURTAINS

_____	❑ ❑	_____	_____	_____	_____
_____	❑ ❑	_____	_____	_____	_____
_____	❑ ❑	_____	_____	_____	_____
_____	❑ ❑	_____	_____	_____	_____
_____	❑ ❑	_____	_____	_____	_____
_____	❑ ❑	_____	_____	_____	_____

CARPETS & FLOOR COVERS

_____	❑ ❑	_____	_____	_____	_____
_____	❑ ❑	_____	_____	_____	_____
_____	❑ ❑	_____	_____	_____	_____
_____	❑ ❑	_____	_____	_____	_____
_____	❑ ❑	_____	_____	_____	_____
_____	❑ ❑	_____	_____	_____	_____

HOUSE LINEN

_____	❑ ❑	_____	_____	_____	_____
_____	❑ ❑	_____	_____	_____	_____
_____	❑ ❑	_____	_____	_____	_____
_____	❑ ❑	_____	_____	_____	_____
_____	❑ ❑	_____	_____	_____	_____
_____	❑ ❑	_____	_____	_____	_____

ITEMS	INSURED Yes No	ORIGINAL COST	DATE OF PURCHASE	REPLACEMENT COST	PHOTOGRAPH ATTACHED
_____	❏ ❏	_____	_____	_____	_____
_____	❏ ❏	_____	_____	_____	_____
_____	❏ ❏	_____	_____	_____	_____
CLOTHING & SHOES					
_____	❏ ❏	_____	_____	_____	_____
_____	❏ ❏	_____	_____	_____	_____
_____	❏ ❏	_____	_____	_____	_____
_____	❏ ❏	_____	_____	_____	_____
_____	❏ ❏	_____	_____	_____	_____
_____	❏ ❏	_____	_____	_____	_____
_____	❏ ❏	_____	_____	_____	_____
_____	❏ ❏	_____	_____	_____	_____
_____	❏ ❏	_____	_____	_____	_____
_____	❏ ❏	_____	_____	_____	_____
PERSONAL EFFECTS					
_____	❏ ❏	_____	_____	_____	_____
_____	❏ ❏	_____	_____	_____	_____
_____	❏ ❏	_____	_____	_____	_____
_____	❏ ❏	_____	_____	_____	_____
_____	❏ ❏	_____	_____	_____	_____
_____	❏ ❏	_____	_____	_____	_____
EQUIPMENT					
Camping					
_____	❏ ❏	_____	_____	_____	_____
_____	❏ ❏	_____	_____	_____	_____
_____	❏ ❏	_____	_____	_____	_____
_____	❏ ❏	_____	_____	_____	_____
_____	❏ ❏	_____	_____	_____	_____
Sports					
_____	❏ ❏	_____	_____	_____	_____
_____	❏ ❏	_____	_____	_____	_____
_____	❏ ❏	_____	_____	_____	_____
_____	❏ ❏	_____	_____	_____	_____
_____	❏ ❏	_____	_____	_____	_____
Boating					
_____	❏ ❏	_____	_____	_____	_____

ITEMS	INSURED Yes No	ORIGINAL COST	DATE OF PURCHASE	REPLACEMENT COST	PHOTOGRAPH ATTACHED
_____	❑ ❑	_____			
_____	❑ ❑	_____	_____	_____	_____
_____	❑ ❑	_____	_____	_____	_____
_____	❑ ❑	_____	_____	_____	_____
_____	❑ ❑	_____	_____	_____	_____

Other

	INSURED Yes No				
_____	❑ ❑	_____	_____	_____	_____
_____	❑ ❑	_____	_____	_____	_____
_____	❑ ❑	_____	_____	_____	_____
_____	❑ ❑	_____	_____	_____	_____
_____	❑ ❑	_____	_____	_____	_____

TOOLS

_____	❑ ❑	_____	_____	_____	_____
_____	❑ ❑	_____	_____	_____	_____
_____	❑ ❑	_____	_____	_____	_____
_____	❑ ❑	_____	_____	_____	_____
_____	❑ ❑	_____	_____	_____	_____

SPECIALTY ITEMS

_____	❑ ❑	_____	_____	_____	_____
_____	❑ ❑	_____	_____	_____	_____
_____	❑ ❑	_____	_____	_____	_____
_____	❑ ❑	_____	_____	_____	_____
_____	❑ ❑	_____	_____	_____	_____

JEWELRY/WATCHES

_____	❑ ❑	_____	_____	_____	_____
_____	❑ ❑	_____	_____	_____	_____
_____	❑ ❑	_____	_____	_____	_____
_____	❑ ❑	_____	_____	_____	_____
_____	❑ ❑	_____	_____	_____	_____

ARTWORK

_____	❑ ❑	_____	_____	_____	_____
_____	❑ ❑	_____	_____	_____	_____
_____	❑ ❑	_____	_____	_____	_____
_____	❑ ❑	_____	_____	_____	_____

_____	❑ ❑	_____	_____	_____	_____

ITEMS	INSURED Yes No	ORIGINAL COST	DATE OF PURCHASE	REPLACEMENT COST	PHOTOGRAPH ATTACHED
HEIRLOOMS					
_____	❑ ❑	_____	_____	_____	_____
_____	❑ ❑	_____	_____	_____	_____
_____	❑ ❑	_____	_____	_____	_____
_____	❑ ❑	_____	_____	_____	_____
_____	❑ ❑	_____	_____	_____	_____
ANTIQUES					
_____	❑ ❑	_____	_____	_____	_____
_____	❑ ❑	_____	_____	_____	_____
_____	❑ ❑	_____	_____	_____	_____
_____	❑ ❑	_____	_____	_____	_____
_____	❑ ❑	_____	_____	_____	_____
COLLECTIONS (Books, stamps, coins)					
_____	❑ ❑	_____	_____	_____	_____
_____	❑ ❑	_____	_____	_____	_____
_____	❑ ❑	_____	_____	_____	_____
_____	❑ ❑	_____	_____	_____	_____
_____	❑ ❑	_____	_____	_____	_____
APPLIANCES (include brand name)					
_____	❑ ❑	_____	_____	_____	_____
_____	❑ ❑	_____	_____	_____	_____
_____	❑ ❑	_____	_____	_____	_____
_____	❑ ❑	_____	_____	_____	_____
_____	❑ ❑	_____	_____	_____	_____
ELECTRONICS (include brand name) TVs/DVDs/VCRs					
_____	❑ ❑	_____	_____	_____	_____
_____	❑ ❑	_____	_____	_____	_____
_____	❑ ❑	_____	_____	_____	_____
_____	❑ ❑	_____	_____	_____	_____
_____	❑ ❑	_____	_____	_____	_____
Stereo equipment					
_____	❑ ❑	_____	_____	_____	_____
_____	❑ ❑	_____	_____	_____	_____

ITEMS	INSURED Yes No	ORIGINAL COST	DATE OF PURCHASE	REPLACEMENT COST	PHOTOGRAPH ATTACHED
_____	❑ ❑	_____	_____	_____	_____
_____	❑ ❑	_____	_____	_____	_____

Computer hardware/software

	INSURED Yes No				
_____	❑ ❑	_____	_____	_____	_____
_____	❑ ❑	_____	_____	_____	_____
_____	❑ ❑	_____	_____	_____	_____
_____	❑ ❑	_____	_____	_____	_____
_____	❑ ❑	_____	_____	_____	_____
_____	❑ ❑	_____	_____	_____	_____

Phones

_____	❑ ❑	_____	_____	_____	_____
_____	❑ ❑	_____	_____	_____	_____
_____	❑ ❑	_____	_____	_____	_____
_____	❑ ❑	_____	_____	_____	_____

Other electronics

_____	❑ ❑	_____	_____	_____	_____
_____	❑ ❑	_____	_____	_____	_____
_____	❑ ❑	_____	_____	_____	_____
_____	❑ ❑	_____	_____	_____	_____

ADDITIONAL INFORMATION

_____	❑ ❑	_____	_____	_____	_____
_____	❑ ❑	_____	_____	_____	_____
_____	❑ ❑	_____	_____	_____	_____
_____	❑ ❑	_____	_____	_____	_____
_____	❑ ❑	_____	_____	_____	_____
_____	❑ ❑	_____	_____	_____	_____

TOTAL REPLACEMENT COST: _____

Location of receipts/proof of ownership _____

Photographs to document rooms in house? (yes or no) _____

Location: _____

Sorted by: _____